9\15

FOSSIL RIDGE PUBLIC LIBRARY DISTRICT

W9-BTQ-812

CULTURES OF THE WORLD
Poland

FOSSIL RIDGE PUBLIC LIBRARY DISTRICT
BRAIDWOOD, IL 60408

Cavendish
Square
New York

Published in 2016 by Cavendish Square Publishing, LLC
243 5th Avenue, Suite 136, New York, NY 10016

Copyright © 2016 by Cavendish Square Publishing, LLC

Third Edition

No part of this publication may be reproduced, stored in a retrieval system, or transmitted in any form or by any means—electronic, mechanical, photocopying, recording, or otherwise—without the prior permission of the copyright owner. Request for permission should be addressed to Permissions, Cavendish Square Publishing, 243 5th Avenue, Suite 136, New York, NY 10016. Tel (877) 980-4450; fax (877) 980-4454.

Website: cavendishsq.com

This publication represents the opinions and views of the author based on his or her personal experience, knowledge, and research. The information in this book serves as a general guide only. The author and publisher have used their best efforts in preparing this book and disclaim liability rising directly or indirectly from the use and application of this book.

CPSIA Compliance Information: Batch #TK
All websites were available and accurate when this book was sent to press.

Library of Congress Cataloging-in-Publication Data
Heale, Jay.
Poland / Jay Heale, Pawel Grajnert, and Debbie Nevins.
pages cm. — (Cultures of the world)
Includes bibliographical references and index.
ISBN 978-1-50260-340-1 (hardcover) ISBN 978-1-50260-341-8 (ebook)
1. Poland—Juvenile literature. I. Grajnert, Paul. II. Nevins, Debbie. III. Title.

DK4147.H4 2016
943.8—dc23

2015010564

Writers, Jay Heale and Pawel Grajnert; Debbie Nevins, third edition
Editorial Director, third edition: David McNamara
Editor, third edition: Debbie Nevins
Art Director, third edition: Jeffrey Talbot
Designer, third edition: Jessica Nevins
Production Manager, third edition: Jennifer Ryder-Talbot
Cover Picture Researcher: Stephanie Flecha
Picture Researcher, third edition: Jessica Nevins

PICTURE CREDITS

The photographs in this book are used with the permission of: Henryk T. Kaiser/Photolibrary/Getty Images, cover; Przemek Klos/Shutterstock.com, 1; kilerus/Shutterstock.com, 3; Mirek Nowaczyk/Shutterstock.com, 5; PETRAS MALUKAS/AFP/Getty Images, 7; Sean Gallup/Getty Images, 8; AKNIOLKA/Shutterstock.com, 9; Patryk Kosmider/Shutterstock.com, 10; Curioso/Shutterstock.com, 11; Dariusz Paciorek/Getty Images, 12; Lukasz Kurbiel/Shutterstock.com, 13; Stanislaw Tokarski/Shutterstock.com, 14; Jacek_Kadaj/Shutterstock.com, 15; Jorg Hackemann/Shutterstock.com, 16; Oleksiy Mark/Shutterstock.com, 17; Pawel Kazmierczak/Shutterstock.com, 18; ppart/Shutterstock.com, 19; Aleksander Bolbot/Shutterstock.com, 20; Pyty/Shutterstock.com, 20; PHOTOCREO Michal Bednarek/Shutterstock.com,21; Pecold/Shutterstock.com, 22; Mariusz Szczygiel/Shutterstock.com, 24; S-F/Shutterstock.com, 25; File:Rzeczpospolita Rozbiory 2.png/Halibutt/Wikimedia Commons, 26; File:Portret Tadeusz Kosciuszko.jpg/ Juliusz Kossak (1824–1899)/Wikimedia Commons, 28; PlusONE/Shutterstock.com, 30; Keystone/Getty Images, 32; Thierry CAMPION/GAMMA/ Gamma-Rapho via Getty Images, 33; Keystone/Getty Images, 35; Keystone/Getty Images, 36; WOJTEK RADWANSKI/AFP/Getty Images, 37; Dariusz Leszczynski/Shutterstock.com, 38; Universal History Archive/UIG via Getty Images, 40; File:Zgromadzenie Narodowe 4 czerwca 2014 Kancelaria Senatu 03.JPG/ Katarzyna Czerwi ska/Wikimedia Commons, 42; File:KPRP 20130131 WG 267 BRONISLAW KOMOROWSKI.jpg/ Wojciech Grz dzi ski/Wikimedia Commons, 43; Carsten Koall/Getty Images, 44; Bartek Sadowski/Bloomberg via Getty Images, 46; Bartek Sadowski/ Bloomberg via Getty Images, 48; Peter Probst/Shutterstock.com, 49; Ulrich Baumgarten via Getty Images, 50; JANEK SKARZYNSKI/AFP/Getty Images, 52; JANEK SKARZYNSKI/AFP/Getty Images, 54; belizar/Shutterstock.com, 56; Jean-Pierre Lescourret/Lonely Planet Images/Getty Images, 58; Stanislaw Tokarski/Shutterstock.com, 59; Tomasz Bidermann/Shutterstock.com, 60; Masson/Shutterstock.com, 61; Sovfoto/UIG via Getty Images, 63; Aleksandra H. Kossowska/Shutterstock.com, 64; Martin Dimitrov/E+/Getty Images, 66; PHOTOCREO Michal Bednarek/Shutterstock.com, 68; AP Photo/Alik Keplicz, 69; Er Creatives Services Ltd/Iconica/Getty Images, 70; wjarek/Shutterstock.com, 71; AP Photo/Alik Keplicz, 72; villorejo/iStock/ Thinkstock, 73; bartosz_zakrzewski/iStock/Thinkstock, 74; Anilah/Shutterstock.com, 75; Pawel Kazmierczak/Shutterstock.com, 76; Keystone/Getty Images, 79; Gianni Ferrari/Cover/Getty Images, 80; JANEK SKARZYNSKI/AFP/Getty Images, 82; Xseon/Shutterstock.com, 83; Mariusz Switulski/ Shutterstock.com, 84; JANEK SKARZYNSKI/AFP/Getty Images, 86; Dariush M/Shutterstock.com, 87; Joymsk140/Shutterstock.com, 88; Tupungato/ Shutterstock.com, 90; WOJTEK RADWANSKI/AFP/Getty Images, 93; RedKoala/Shutterstock.com, 94; anandoart/Shutterstock.com, 96; Aleksey Stemmer/ Shutterstock.com, 97; Marcin Krzyzak/Shutterstock.com, 98; JANEK SKARZYNSKI/AFP/Getty Images, 99; David Corio/Redferns/Getty Images, 100; Kevin Winter/Getty Images, 101; karnizz/Shutterstock.com, 102; Agnes Kantaruk/Shutterstock.com, 103; IgorXIII/Shutterstock.com, 104; Tata2anka/ Shutterstock.com, 106; Dziurek/Shutterstock.com, 108; Dziurek/Shutterstock.com, 109; Mike Hewitt/Getty Images, 110; marekusz/Shutterstock.com, 111; Olaf Protze/LightRocket via Getty Images, 112; Pablo77/Shutterstock.com, 114; Michal Ludwiczak/Shutterstock.com, 116; Pawel Kazmierczak/ Shutterstock.com, 117; JANEK SKARZYNSKI/AFP/Getty Images, 118; JANEK SKARZYNSKI/AFP/Getty Images, 119; Witold Skrypczak/Lonely Planet Images/Getty Images, 120; Curioso/Shutterstock.com, 122; Teresa Kasprzycka/Shutterstock.com, 124; Malgorzata Kistryn/Shutterstock.com, 125; Ice Cherry/Shutterstock.com, 126; bozulek/Shutterstock.com, 127; Dar1930/Shutterstock.com, 128; JANEK SKARZYNSKI/AFP/Getty Images, 129; mffoto/ Shutterstock.com, 130; Razmarinka/Shutterstock.com, 131.

PRECEDING PAGE

A little girl jumps on stones with the Tatra Mountains in the background.

Printed in the United States of America

CONTENTS

POLAND TODAY

SOME PEOPLE SAY POLAND IS A BLEAK AND DEPRESSING PLACE—
some Poles themselves even say so.

Given the country's turbulent history, such an assessment might have been understandable in the past. But is it still true today?

The Polish flag is red and white, but perhaps it should be black and blue, for all the beatings the country has endured. Poland has been squeezed, squashed, slashed, and stolen—and literally wiped off the map. It has been patched back together only to be brutalized by occupying forces—first by German Nazis during World War II, and then by the Soviet Union after the war.

The Nazis chose Poland as the place to build their factories of death. In a few short years, they killed off six million Poles, including three million Polish Jews—almost the entire Jewish population. For those Poles who didn't die, the pure terror of living had to have lasting effects on the national character.

After the Nazis, what little life was left in Poland's veins would be further sucked out by yet another bloodthirsty ideology. Soviet Communism brought a bleak, gray, dehumanizing uniformity to Polish society; a life of grim weariness, of having to stand

Crowds of faithful watch the canonization ceremony of Pope John Paul II on April 27, 2014.

on one long line for bread, and then on another long line for meat, only to find the provisions had run out. Poles were shut up and shut off from the rest of the world, feeling forgotten.

And yet, look what happened: Adolf Hitler's Third Reich went up in smoke. The Germans lost the war, Hitler died, and the Nazis were, and still are, hunted to the corners of the Earth. The Soviet Union crumbled, literally piece by piece, as the Communist economy failed. And there stands Poland, having emerged from the ashes of the twentieth century like a phoenix. Pope John Paul II—the first ever Polish pope—inspired a new spirit of hope and resistance in his fellow Poles, and Lech Walesa's Solidarity movement brought a feisty new energy to the country. Poland turned around, looked to the West, and saw its future.

In 1999, a short decade after the collapse of Communism, Poland joined the North Atlantic Treaty Organization (NATO), along with its neighbors and former Warsaw Pact members, Hungary and the Czech Republic. NATO is a military alliance of nations in Europe and North America dedicated to collective and mutual defense. Member states are required to come to the aid of any member state that is subject to an armed attack. The Warsaw Pact had been a similar organization of Communist states in Eastern and Central Europe.

In light of Russia's military interference, beginning in 2014, in Ukraine—which is not a NATO member—Poland and its NATO neighbors must have felt their quick leap to align with the West was justified. Western leaders thought so as well. In September 2014, for example, United Kingdom Prime Minister David Cameron emphasized NATO's role in holding back Russian aggression. He said, "It is very important when Russians look at countries like Estonia or Latvia or Poland that they don't just see Estonian, Latvian, and Polish soldiers—they see French, German, British soldiers too."

Poland went further. In 2004, it joined the European Union, an economic union of European countries with the purpose of establishing a single market. The EU enforces common standards in areas such as human rights, democracy, environmental policies, and so forth. For Poland, this has meant having to pull itself up to the higher level of these mostly Western European standards, a difficult task given the backward condition the country found itself in at the end of the twentieth century.

By almost any measure, Poland's rehabilitation and reinvention, though not yet complete, has been an astonishing success. It used EU monies to build hundreds of miles of new highways, modern sewerage systems, youth sports facilities, and kindergartens and pre-schools. Meanwhile, its economy boomed; its GDP per capita (a measure of a country's productivity) rose from 44 percent of the EU average in 2004 to 67 percent of the EU average in 2014. It is forecast to reach 74 percent by 2020.

Membership in the EU has benefitted Poland in many noneconomic ways as well. Poland has become a more open society, more in tune with the outside world, and more tolerant and accepting of other peoples and cultures—in a word, it has become more European. The nearly all-white

Poles take "selfies" as they eat Polish apples. It's part of a campaign to show Russian president Vladimir Putin that they do not fear him. In 2014, Putin banned the importation of apples and other Polish goods to Russia after Poland condemned Russian interference in Ukraine.

Polish president
Bronisław
Komorowski
speaks at the
anniversary
ceremony marking
the liberation of
the Auschwitz-
Birkenau
concentration
camps.

country has, to a large extent, embraced Western culture and its changing attitudes and values.

Some observers say the past twenty-five years have been Poland's best in many centuries. Radek Sikorski, Poland's minister of foreign affairs from 2007 to 2014, said in a 2013 magazine interview, "The twentieth century was a roller coaster for Poland, regaining independence after World War I, then losing it and getting ethnically cleansed by Stalin and Hitler together, and then forty-five years of struggle for democracy. Hopefully, we'll produce less history than in the past. Geopolitically, we are having the best time in three hundred years. And we are now contributing to other countries' stability, being a source of European solutions."

Poland today is a generally optimistic and forward-looking country. Who could blame the Poles for not wanting to look back at their nation's grim past? That past is never very far beneath the surface, however, and old bones have a way of rattling when justice remains incomplete.

In January 2015, about three hundred survivors of the Auschwitz concentration camp in Poland returned to commemorate the seventieth anniversary of the camp's liberation. People with living memories of the

Holocaust's most infamous death camps are mostly gone now. These survivors, people in their eighties and nineties, were children and teens when they were held prisoners there. World leaders, including the presidents of Poland, Germany, Austria, and France, also participated in the ceremonies.

The commemoration was just one way that Poland is trying to come to terms with its complicated past. In addition, archaeologists are literally digging up those unquiet bones from mass graves in various locations: the Treblinka Death Camp, the Bialystok Detention Center, abandoned Jewish cemeteries, and other places that harbor history's grisly secrets. One of the saddest secrets is this: as much as the Polish people suffered, resisted, and fought their oppressors, there were, of course, some who collaborated with the enemy. The 2014 Academy Award for Best Foreign Film went to the Polish movie *Ida*, a film about that uncomfortable truth.

For Poland, putting the past to rest will only speed the way to a happier future, the beginning of what some predict will be a "New Golden Age" for the country. As Poland's Nobel prize-winning poet Wislawa Szymborska says in "The End and the Beginning" (2001), her famous poem about how a country comes back to life after a war:

A tiny citizen looks to the future with optimism.

> Those who knew
> what was going on here
> must make way for
> those who know little.
> And less than little.
> And finally as little as nothing.

Poland today is doing just that. Welcome to Poland!

GEOGRAPHY

The Eye of the Sea Lake in Poland's Tatra Mountains reflects the beauty of its surroundings.

1

POLAND'S MOUNTAINS AND LAKES are its most dramatic features, but most of the country is made up of spreading plains, dominated by green miles of woods, parks, and small strip-field farms. Elsewhere, however, are less scenic views: gray zones of apartment blocks, houses of unplastered concrete bricks, and industrial hulks from the Communist past.

Poland has a desert, which is highly unusual in that part of the world. The Bledow Desert, nicknamed "The Polish Sahara," is a sandy expanse left behind by an ancient glacier. The desert is also the result of human activity—centuries of mining which lowered the ground's water table, killing off plant life, and revealing the sands beneath.

Poland's Bledow Desert is an unusual geographic phenomenon.

Poland is a squarish area of land that stretches from the Baltic Sea in the north to the Carpathian Mountains in the south. Poland's neighbors are: Germany to the west; the Czech Republic and Slovakia to the south; Ukraine and Belarus to the east; and Lithuania and Russia to the northeast. With a total area of 120,728 square miles (312,684 square km), Poland is the ninth largest country in Europe.

Most of Poland is part of the northern European plain. More than 75 percent of the land is less than 650 feet (198 m) above sea level. Poland's largest rivers, the Vistula and the Oder, originate in the Carpathian Mountains and wind north across the plains to the Baltic Sea. The central and northern areas are rather sandy and infertile. About 60 percent of the land is farmed, and more than a quarter is covered by forests.

The capital of Poland is Warsaw, slightly to the east of the country's geographical center. In the north are the Masurian Lakes; northwest the Baltic coast; southwest the region called Silesia; and south, bordering the Czech Republic and Slovakia, the Tatra and Sudety ranges.

The Oder River flows north through the western part of Poland.

SIX CLEAR SEASONS

Geography books describe Poland's climate as temperate in the west and continental in the east. (A temperate climate is one in which temperatures are moderate, without extreme swings of hot and cold. A continental climate is relatively dry with very hot summers and very cold winters.) Warm air blows in from the Atlantic Ocean, far to the west, while cold polar air blows in from Russia to the east. Climatic conditions are especially important in Poland, as much of the country depends on local agriculture.

Crocuses bloom in the Chocholowska Valley of the Tatra Mountains.

Poland has six identifiable seasons. Cold, snowy winter breaks into early spring; then comes spring, sunny and flower-filled. The short summer, with plenty of rain and sunshine, can be quite hot in the big cities. Summer is followed by the warm, golden fall, with rich colors everywhere. Then, a foggy, humid period heralds the approach of winter. Winter can be bleak in the central plains, so people throng south to the ski slopes of the Tatra Mountain resorts.

The temperature ranges from 76°F (24.4°C) or higher in summer to 20°F (-6.7°C) in the mountains in winter. The record low was -41.1°F (-40.6°C) in 1929, while the record high was 104.4°F (40.2°C) in 1921. The Baltic region is sunniest in summer, while the Carpathian Mountains receive the most sunshine in winter. Annual rainfall ranges from 31 to 47 inches (78.7 to 119.4 cm) in the mountains to 18 inches (45.7 cm) in the middle Polish lowlands, for an annual average of 24 inches (61 cm).

A CARPET OF FIELDS

From the air, much of Poland looks like a carpet of narrow fields and meadows colored with the bright yellow of rapeseed, the warm ochre of wheat and rye, and the fresh green of potato plants—like a patchwork quilt made of thin parallel strips but without any dividing fences.

This aerial view shows the patchwork effect of farm fields near the Vistula River.

Before World War I, much of Poland's agricultural land was owned by rich landowners and worked by laborers. When the Communists took power, the government tried to enforce a policy of collective farms. The Poles bitterly resisted the idea of joint ownership and the sharing of proceeds. Only about one-fifth of Polish farmland was collectivized. While young people worked in towns, older people stayed on the farms, so the countryside did not change much. But since Poland became a member of the European Union in 2004, modernization and urbanization has been displacing many of the smaller farmers who cannot afford to upgrade to meet the new EU standards. Those farmers have switched to subsistence farming, growing only as much as they need to feed their own families. But for larger, more modern farms, joining the EU has been a boon, tripling farm incomes.

Their largest crop is wheat, amounting to some 12.2 million tons (11.1 million tonnes) in 2014—2015. Poland's other crops include rye, barley, oats, sugar beets, fruit such as blueberries, strawberries, and blackcurrants, and vegetables such as potatoes, cabbages, onions, and beets. Oak, pine, and birch trees line country roads. Pine makes up more than half of the forested land, along with larch and beech, and spruce fir on the mountain slopes.

TWO IMPORTANT CITIES

WARSAW Stories say that a mermaid once lived in the Vistula, the greatest river in Poland. This mythical being is now found on Warsaw's coat of arms. This historic city is now surrounded by seemingly endless gray housing estates. Fortunately, the busy roads lead straight to the more attractive modern city center, built around the landmark Palace of Culture and Science. The more historic parts of Warsaw, as well as the newer residential areas, are on the Vistula's western bank. The eastern bank, the Praga, escaped war damage because the Red Army occupied it before the Nazis were able to level it as they did the rest of Warsaw.

The column of Zygmund III Wasa, the king who moved Poland's royal capital from Krakow to Warsaw in 1596, stands in the center of Castle Square. The statue is Warsaw's oldest monument and was the first to be rebuilt after World War II. In the square, horses clip-clop on the cobblestones, pulling carriages past open-air cafés, artists, souvenir and flower stalls, and camera-toting tourists.

Sundown over Warsaw shows off the city's skyline.

Tourists visit the Royal Castle, with its beautifully restored interior, the Historical Museum, and the Cathedral of Saint John—the scene of some of the most bitter fighting in the Warsaw Uprising in 1944, when more than 250,000 Polish soldiers and civilians were killed during two months of street fighting with the Nazis. Around 85 percent of the city was destroyed. South of the city is the Wilanow Palace, once the summer residence of Jan III Sobieski, a seventeenth-century Polish king. Visitors to the palace wear felt slippers, obligatory in all Polish museums, as they view superbly painted walls and ceilings, and admire the formal gardens.

KRAKOW Krakow stands where the Tatra Mountains join the Polish Plain. The former capital is home to the country's oldest university, Jagiellonian, founded in 1364. Krakow is a completely preserved medieval city, one of only a few Polish cities to escape the devastation of World War II. It is listed by UNESCO as one of the world's twelve most significant historic sites. Krakow's main market square, Rynek Glowny, is Europe's largest square. Cafés, beer gardens, and restaurants line all sides of the square, which serves as

People enjoy a fine day in May at a park by the Vistula River in the historic center of Krakow.

A CITY REBUILT

At the end of World War II, Warsaw lay in ruins, a victim of systematic Nazi destruction. In a strangely uncharacteristic mood, the new Communist rulers chose to rebuild old Warsaw rather than replace it with cheap, stark Stalinist housing projects. So, working from old prints and paintings, this historic city was painstakingly reconstructed. Paintings of eighteenth-century Warsaw, saved from the burning ruins of the former Royal Castle, served as architectural models. Twenty million tons of rubble were removed and turned into building material. One hundred carloads of rubble were removed every day. Women and high-school students helped in the rebuilding.

Today, the warm pastel colors of Warsaw's Old Town have been preserved, and the past has not been forgotten. Memorial plaques everywhere describe mass executions of civilians, and bullet holes can be seen in the few original sections of the rebuilt houses. Today the city center has been deemed a World Heritage Site.

a location for local cultural displays. Flower sellers surround the medieval Cloth Hall, now a covered market full of booths selling folk art and typical Polish souvenirs. In a corner of the square stands the magnificent Church of Our Lady Mary.

Wawel Hill, standing on a bend of the Vistula River, is one of the historical gems of Poland. Here the Royal Castle of Wawel sits high on a hill above the Vistula. Rebuilt at the end of the sixteenth century, the castle boasts a great courtyard and a crypt where Polish kings lie entombed in massive marble. All but four of Poland's forty-five monarchs are buried in the Wawel Royal Cathedral. Long lines of visitors walk through rooms decorated in colored marble and priceless Flemish tapestries. One can see such treasures as a jewel-studded shield captured from the Turks at the battle of Vienna in 1683,

A chair lift on Kasprowy Wierch, a mountain in Zakopane, overlooks the Gasienicowa Valley in the distance.

a velvet hat with a dove embroidered in pearls (given to Jan III Sobieski by the pope after Vienna was saved), and a dazzling robe embroidered with heraldic suns (a gift to Sobieski by French King Louis XIV).

Legend has it that a dragon lived in a cave beneath Wawel Hill. Krak, the mythical founder of Krakow, commissioned the slaying of the terrible beast to save his daughter, who was to be sacrificed to the dragon. A humble shoemaker devised a way to kill the beast by feeding it animal skins stuffed with tar and sulfur. The dragon gobbled them up, was driven into a frenzy of thirst, rushed into the Vistula, and drank until it exploded.

MOUNTAIN RANGES

Poland's southern boundary is formed by a chain of mountain ranges. Snowcapped for much of the year, the High Tatras are the most famous and most popular. Their alpine-style heights offer outdoor adventure for skiers in winter and for hikers and climbers in summer. Rising beyond 8,100 feet

(2,469 m), the High Tatras are part of the Carpathian Mountains that straddle Poland, the Czech Republic, and Slovakia.

Farther east, the Pieniny Mountains are cut by the Dunajec River, and to the southwest stands the Beskidy range, picturesque with spruce and beech forests, the source of the Vistula River, which flows across the Polish plain. The mountains not only provide recreation but also support the important forestry industry. The foothills of the Tatra Mountains are called the Podhale (pod-HA-le)—a sparsely populated area of lush meadows. The main town there is Nowy Targ, known for its market that starts at 3 a.m. every Thursday. Deeper into the Tatra Mountains, past steep valleys and quaint villages carved lovingly from the local timber, stands Zakopane, a little mountain town that attracts visitors from all over Poland. It is also a gathering place for artists.

Sunbathers enjoy a day at the beach on the Baltic Sea in Niechorze, Poland.

BALTIC COAST

Poland has a 430-mile (692 km) coastline on the Baltic Sea. Poland's annual catch of fish is 225,000 tons (204,000 metric tons). There are good fishing grounds in the Baltic for cod and herring, but pollution has killed off some species of fish, such as sturgeon.

In the seventeenth century, Gdansk was more than twice Warsaw's size. Formerly an independent city-state known as Danzig, Gdansk had a multiethnic, multi-religious population consisting mainly of Germans, Dutch, Poles, Kaszubians, and Scandinavians. Gdansk, along with other cities, suffered greatly during World War II. The Russians destroyed 90 percent of Gdansk when they "liberated" the town after the German occupation. Gdansk was the birthplace of the free trade union Solidarity.

Once upon a time, the vast European Plain was covered in forest. This was the deep, dense forest of European fairy tales; and earlier still, by thousands of years, was even home to lions, elephants, and rhinos! Almost all of that original forest is gone now, having been cleared for centuries by humans for agriculture and civilization. That doesn't mean Europe has no forests; today about 35 percent of Europe is covered in woodlands, but they are relatively new-growth forests. But there is one place where the primeval forest remains, and a good part of it is in Poland.

Straddling the border of Poland and Belarus, the wild, ancient Bialowieza Forest is a reminder of the Europe that once was. Today, on Poland's side, it is a national park of more than 300,000 acres (121,406 hectares). (On the much larger Belarus side, it is the Belovezhskaya Pushcha National Park.)

The forest was once home to one of the world's last wild bison herds, but during World War I, hungry soldiers killed all the bison. In 1929 three pairs of bison were brought to the forest from foreign zoos, and today about nine hundred European bison, Europe's heaviest land animal, now roam freely. Deer, wildcats, lynx, wolves, and beaver also live under the great green cathedral, where huge spruce trees reach 150 feet (45.7 m). Some ancient oaks are so large and so old, they have been given names. The Tsar Oak, for example, on the Belarussian side is more than eight hundred years old.

Because the forest has been relatively undisturbed, it supports a rich diversity of wildlife, including fifty-nine mammal species, along with more than 250 bird, thirteen amphibian, seven reptile and more than twelve thousand invertebrate species. For its future protection, the forest has been named a UNESCO World Heritage Site and Biosphere Reserve.

Gdansk is linked by urban development to its neighbors Sopot and Gdynia, forming what is known as the Tri-City. The polluted waters of the Vistula enter the sea here, affecting the whole bay of Gdansk.

To the east lie the Masurian Lakes, a popular summer destination for sailing and swimming. The main launching point for canoeists and forest hikers is the town of Olsztyn.

Red roofs shine at sunset in the Old Town section of Gdansk on the Motlawa River.

INTERNET LINKS

travel.nationalgeographic.com/travel/countries/poland-guide
National Geographic's Poland Guide has feature stories, photo galleries, and a map.

whc.unesco.org/en/list/30
The UNESCO page for the Historic Center of Warsaw, a World Heritage Site, explains the history and importance of the city.

bpn.com.pl/index.php?lang=en
The website of the Bialowieza National Park has many sections in English, including information about the European bison.

whc.unesco.org/en/list/33
The UNESCO World Heritage site's page about the Bialowieza Forest explains why it is so valuable.

HISTORY

Bedzin Castle dates to the fourteenth century; the town of Bedzin, in southern Poland, dates to the ninth century.

2

From 2006 to 2007, the president and prime minister of Poland were identical twin brothers, Lech Kaczynski and Jaroslaw Kaczynski.

THE HISTORY OF POLAND IS A LONG and powerful story. It is a tale of a people fighting for freedom and independence, over and over again, against foreign domination. Squeezed between strong, aggressive neighbors, Poland has been redrawn on the map many times—chopped up, partitioned, and literally shifted to the west. It has gone from being the largest country in Europe to disappearing completely for more than a century. The Polish people have suffered horribly in war after war, but their gritty resilience has ensured the survival, and rebirth, of Poland for a millennium.

The story begins with the Slavic tribes that lived in the Vistula River Basin. In the ninth century CE, several West Slavic tribes united to form small states. One was ruled by the Piast dynasty, which by the mid-900s had united the region surrounding present-day Poznan. In 966, considered the year of Poland's founding, Piast ruler Mieszko I adopted Christianity. During his rule, tribes speaking similar languages were united.

At that time, local noblemen kept private armies, and the countryside was divided into dukedoms and principalities often in conflict with one

another. But by 1109 Poland was strong enough to defend against invasions by Germanic tribes from the west, and a network of castles was built to defend the borders. By the fourteenth century, Poland was a united kingdom that stretched from the Baltic Sea to the Black Sea. When it united with Lithuania in the sixteenth century, Poland was the largest country in Europe.

INVASIONS

The geographical position of Poland, spread across the northern plains between Europe and Asia, made it an easy path for invaders. The Mongol armies of Genghis Khan left trails of terror and destruction in the thirteenth century, as the knights of Europe were no match for them. The Mongols did not conquer Europe, although they did invade twice that century, burning most Polish cities.

The Teutonic Knights, German Crusaders who had originally been organized to provide charity and take care of the sick in the Holy Land, eventually grew into a powerful and cruel military force. In 1308 the Teutonic Knights snatched the lands of Pomerania—coastal territory on the Baltic Sea, cutting Poland off from the sea. That started 150 years of warfare with Poland that eventually led to the Knights' decline.

The ruins of Ogrodzieniec Castle are said to be haunted by a spector of the fifteenth-century nobleman, Stanislaw Warszycki.

FENDING OFF ATTACKS

In 1569, the Union of Lublin Kingdom of Poland united the Grand Duchy of Lithuania with the Kingdom of Poland, creating the Poland-Lithuania Commonwealth. In the sixteenth and seventeenth centuries, it was the largest country in Europe. In 1558 Tsar Ivan IV (the Terrible) of Russia invaded Livonia (present-day Latvia and Estonia). Poland-Lithuania intervened, and in 1582 Polish King Stefan Batory (r. 1576—1586) defeated the Russians.

In the center of Krakow rise the two Gothic towers of Saint Mary's Church. The towers are uneven. Legend has it that they were built by two brothers, one of whom murdered the other so that his tower would be the highest. His murder weapon, a knife, hangs in the Cloth Hall, another historic building in Krakow.

The higher tower is home to the Krakow Trumpeter, whose tale is yet another legend (which is probably not based on fact). The story goes that in 1241, a young trumpeter sounded the alarm when the Mongol Tartar forces began burning the city, but an arrow pierced his throat, cutting off his trumpet call. So when the anthem sounds today, the last note breaks off abruptly. Even during the German occupation, the trumpet sounded "every hour of the day and night." Men from the Polish fire brigade still swear the ancient oath to "sound the Heynal (HAY-now) each hour in honor of Our Lady in the tower of the church which bears Her Name." Tradition dictates that the Heynal be played each hour on the hour, "four times to the four winds."

But in 1655 the Swedes invaded Poland, and their occupation lasted five years. In the following decade, Poland fended off more attacks by the Russians and the Ottoman Turks, losing territory.

In 1674 Jan III Sobieski was elected king of Poland. He made a pact with Leopold I of Austria, who in 1683 called on Sobieski to save Vienna. Reinforcing the army of Charles V, the duke of Lorraine, Sobieski drove back the invading Turks, and was heralded as the savior of Christian Europe.

Polish greatness declined after Sobieski's death in Warsaw in 1696. Weakened by wars with the Turks, disagreements among the nobles, and quarrels at the election of every king, Poland became prey to the greater powers of Europe, namely Russia, Prussia, and Austria.

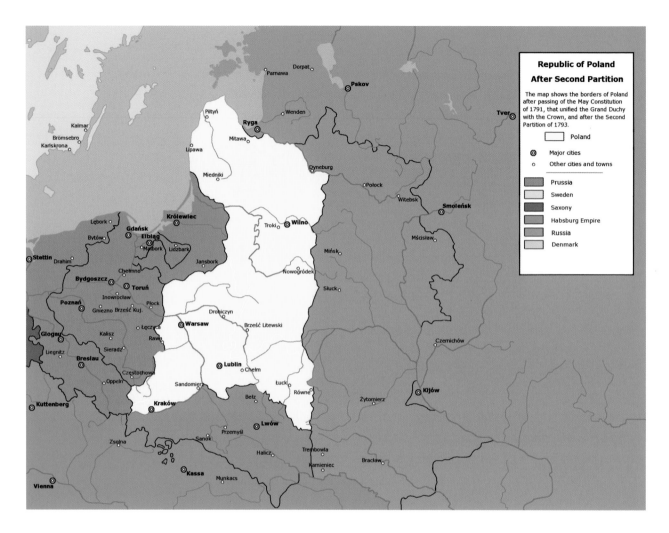

Republic of Poland

After Second Partition

The map shows the borders of Poland after passing of the May Constitution of 1791, that unified the Grand Duchy with the Crown, and after the Second Partition of 1793.

☐ Poland

◎ Major cities

○ Other cities and towns

▨ Prussia

▨ Sweden

▨ Saxony

▨ Habsburg Empire

▨ Russia

▨ Denmark

The map shows Poland as it existed at the time of the second partition, around the time it established its new constitution.

THE END OF POLAND

In 1772 came the first of three partitions that would eventually erase Poland from the map. Russia, Austria-Hungary, and Prussia seized large portions of Polish territory. Jolted into action, Poland improved its education system and, encouraged by a wave of fresh political thinking, pushed government reforms. In 1791 Poland adopted a new constitution, becoming only the second country in the world, after the United States, to do so.

The envisaged consolidation of royal power and political reorganization brought fierce opposition from Russia, which sent troops into Poland in 1792.

The constitution was abolished in 1793, and a second partition was made between Russia and Prussia.

After an uprising in Warsaw, Krakow, and Wilno (Vilnius), in 1795 Russia, Austria-Hungary, and Prussia claimed the last of Poland, which was already a Russian protectorate. Poland disappeared from the map for more than a century.

FOREIGN RULE

During the nineteenth century, Polish lands were under the rule of Imperial Russia or the Prussians. After a failed uprising against Russian rule by Polish nationalists in 1831, Russia abolished Polish self-governance and civil liberties. Uprisings against Russian rule in 1846, 1848, and 1863 led to harsh measures at "Russification," or the imposing of Russian culture on the conquered people.

"Germanization"—the imposition of German culture—was the rule in Prussian-controlled areas, but the treatment was not as harsh. After the fall of Imperial Russia in 1917, Germany gained control over Russian-held Polish territory. A provisional Polish government was set up in Paris, and the Germans created a regency council for the Polish "kingdom."

POLAND, REBORN

During World War I, US president Woodrow Wilson declared that restoring a reunited, independent Poland was a resolute aim of the Allies. After the Allied victory, Polish independence was proclaimed on November 11, 1918, by Jozef Pilsudski, the founder of the Polish Legions that fought against Germany. On June 28, 1919, the Treaty of Versailles officially recognized Polish independence, although more fighting was to come. In 1920 Poland's attempt to seize Ukraine led to an attack by Russia's Red Army, which soon moved toward Warsaw. Pilsudski led the Polish army in a successful counterattack. Under the Treaty of Riga, Russia ceded a large part of Ukraine to Poland, whose eastern border was fixed on the Zbrucz River. In 1921 the Second Polish Republic adopted the March Constitution, which declared

Tadeusz Kosciuszko (ta-deh-OOSH kusht-YOOSH-shkoh) (1746–1817) was a Polish military engineer who became a national hero in both Poland and the United States. Born in a village in the Polish-Lithuanian Commonwealth, he studied in France and moved to North America in 1776. The American Revolutionary War was raging and Kosciuszko became a colonel in the Continental Army, fighting against the British. As a military architect, he designed and oversaw the construction of defense fortifications at West Point, along the Hudson River in New York State. In 1783, he was promoted to brigadier general.

He returned to Poland the following year, however, and fought for his homeland as a major general in the Polish-Lithuanian Commonwealth Army. This was during the time of the partitioning of Poland. After the Second Partition in 1794, in which Russia and Prussia helped themselves to huge chunks of Poland, Kosciuszko organized and led an uprising of 6,200 men against Russia. At the Battle of Maciejowice, Russian forces destroyed the Poles, and injured and then captured Kosciuszko. He valiantly tried to kill himself at that moment only to find his pistol was out of ammunition.

The Russian troops went on to slaughter twenty thousand Warsaw residents and soon the Third Partition of 1795 ate up what remained of Poland. Kosciuszko, who had

been taken to Russia, was pardoned by the czar. He moved back to America, where he became a close friend of Thomas Jefferson. Being a lifelong advocate for human rights, Kosciuszko drew up a will directing that the money from his American estate be used for the purpose of the education and freedom of US slaves. The Polish war hero died in Switzerland in 1817, but his American assets were never used for the purpose he expressed.

Today there are a number of memorials, museums, cities, bridges, and streets named after Kosciuszko in both Poland and the United States—and even a mountain in Australia that bears his name.

Poland's sovereignty. However, the years following were plagued by political instability. In 1926 Pilsudski seized power in a military coup and governed until his death in 1935.

WORLD WAR II

On the false pretext that the Polish state was somehow abusing German nationals in and around the city of *Danzig* (Gdansk), the Nazis invaded Poland. World War II began at 4:45 a.m. on September 1, 1939, when the German naval vessel *Schleswig-Holstein* bombarded the Polish defensive positions on Westerplatte, an ammunition depot just outside Gdansk. Almost simultaneously, German armored divisions crossed the border into Poland from the west. On September 17, the Red Army invaded in the east. Polish forces fought until September 27, when Warsaw fell. Military aid promised by France and Great Britain never arrived. After a fierce thirty-six-day campaign, Poland was once again divided between Germany and Russia.

Then began a reign of terror. Hitler wanted racial purity in his widening empire and regarded Poles as subhuman. Those considered at odds with German policy were put into concentration camps, which became death camps. Russia depopulated its share of Poland by deporting between one million and two million Poles in cattle trucks to Siberia and other Russian territories. An underground organization called the Home Army, which consistedof more than 300,000 people, destroyed German communications, blew up bridges, and hindered production of war materials through the entire occupation. In Paris, a Polish government-in-exile was formed in 1939. It later moved to London.

NEW BOUNDARIES

By the time Germany fell on May 8, 1945, Poland had lost around six million citizens, the capital was obliterated, and survivors were impoverished. In a post-war peace treaty, the Potsdam Agreement of 1945, the United States, the United Kingdom, and the Soviet Union redrew the national borders of Poland and some of its neighbors. Poland was essentially shifted to the

"(Tadeusz Kosciuszko) is as pure a son of liberty as I have ever known."
—Thomas Jefferson (1743–1826), third US president

Poland bears the heavy burden of being the location of the most infamous of the Nazi concentration camps: Majdanek, Treblinka, and Auschwitz-Birkenau. The camps' specific purpose was the destruction of a nation and the annihilation of a people. Hitler's "Final Solution" turned Poland into a mass graveyard.

Auschwitz, previously a Polish military barracks, became a labor camp for Poles who were considered anti-Nazi. The cynical motto over the gate reads Arbeit Macht Frei

("Work Makes You Free"). Auschwitz was later turned into a station for Jews on their way to the death camp in Birkenau. Today, this horrifying site serves as a museum. On display are piles of personal belongings looted from Jewish families before they were murdered. In the barracks, there is a mountain of human hair shorn from

victims, with some material woven from it; there are also empty canisters that once contained Zyklon-B, the hydrogen cyanide compound used to kill inmates.

Block 10 housed the women who were used as subjects in medical experiments. Block 11 was the prison within a prison. Inmates accused of serious offences were dumped in tiny, damp basement cells, too small to sit or even squat in. Political prisoners were tried and executed.

Birkenau (Auschwitz II) was built as a factory devoted to death. The gas chambers were disguised as huge shower rooms, where more than a million—probably far more— Polish Jews were massacred. Their bodies were at first buried but later burned. Crematoria were constructed to incinerate more than four thousand bodies in twenty-four hours. Toward the end of the war, the Nazis destroyed much of Birkenau to try to keep its grim secrets from being discovered.

In January 2015, Poland commemorated the seventieth anniversary of the liberation of the Auschwitz concentration camps in a ceremony attended by many world leaders.

west, losing a large part of its eastern territory to the Soviets, but gaining a significant chunk of land to its west from Germany. Large segments of the German and Polish populations were transferred or resettled as well. The result was a new Poland made up of a largely homogenous, ethnically Polish population.

A COMMUNIST STATE

Poland's new government formed under the oversight—or domination—of the Soviet Union, as the major world powers had agreed to in the post-war treaties. Poland therefore became a Communist state. The Communist Party wielded all the power in the new "People's Republic," and Communist policy stated that "the land now belongs to the peasants."

Almost every major city except Krakow had to be rebuilt, but in Communist ideology, top priority was given to the building of steel, coal, iron, and armaments industries. Poland joined the Warsaw Pact, the Communist alliance. Daily life became a nightmare under the Soviet regime. People suspected of being hostile to the state were denounced, arrested, and executed without trial. Children were encouraged to inform on their parents. The Roman Catholic Church was openly attacked, but the majority of people remained devoutly Catholic.

In efforts to win Polish support, the Soviet regime promoted free education and social security. Cheap books were published that were available to all, and food costs were subsidized. But the failure of the Soviet's Six-Year Plan (1950—1955), which focused on developing heavy industry and collectivizing agriculture, created increasing economic disaster and social discontent. Industrial workers rioted in Poznan with the slogan "No bread without freedom."

THE BEGINNING OF FREEDOM

October 19, 1956, marked a showdown between Poland's and Russia's Communist party leaders, Wladyslaw Gomulka and Nikita Khrushchev. Gomulka, who refused to be bullied into subservience to Russia's

Polish President Wladyslaw Gomulka (*right*), meets with Soviet Premier Nikita Khrushchev (*left*) at the United Nations in New York City.

Communist hierarchy, was re-elected that day in Warsaw as the first secretary. The only remaining Communist of importance still popular in Poland, he received messages of support from miners, steelworkers, and labor unions. He needed all the help he could muster.

Russian troops had surrounded Warsaw. Top Russian officials had flown in and were at the Belvedere Palace, where the re-election took place. The crowd at the event witnessed the confrontation between the two leaders, as Khrushchev threatened to use force if Gomulka did not comply with Russia's demands. Gomulka responded by telling the crowd what those demands were. He reminded the Russians of the economic collapse, growing Polish resentment, Russian economic exploitation, and Russia's failure to repatriate some 500,000 Poles held captive since the war.

Early the next morning, the negotiations drew to a close. A weary Gomulka told his supporters to go home, as the Russians left Warsaw. The Poles went wild, and cheering crowds filled the streets. Gomulka presented the nation with a virtual declaration of independence from Russia: "Poland has the right to be sovereign, and this sovereignty must be respected."

But by summer, the economic crisis had become so acute that the government could not maintain food subsidies. Price increases were proposed, leading to strikes and protests, which were met by police brutality and arrests. About two thousand people were detained, many savagely beaten in custody.

STARVATION AND STRIKES

Gomulka had gained three concessions: the Church's independence, freedom from state-controlled agriculture, and some political freedom. But Polish Communism resulted in near starvation for much of Poland. A food price hike in 1970 drove Polish workers to strike, and a proposed price increase in 1976 provoked more strikes.

In 1980 the Polish government made another attempt to raise food prices to a more sustainable level. Shipyard strikes paralyzed the country, forcing the authorities to give in to the workers' demands for wage increases, free labor unions, and the release of political prisoners. It was a severe embarrassment to the government. Concessions reluctantly offered by the deputy prime minister were not approved by the Politburo, the Communist party's principal policy-making and executive committee. Members of the workers' opposition, the Workers Defense Committee, were detained; the editor of *Robotnik* (*The Worker*), an underground publication, was arrested and beaten. With most of the Baltic coast workforce on strike by then, the government recognized Solidarity, an organization of free trade unions.

SOLIDARITY LIVES!

Solidarity (*Solidarnosc*) was the first free labor union in the Communist bloc. In December 1981, General Wojciech Jaruzelski (who earlier that year succeeded Edward Gierek, who in 1970 succeeded Gomulka) declared martial law and banned Solidarity. Its members were arrested or killed, and its leader, Lech Walesa, was locked up in a remote hunting lodge. Meanwhile, food shortages increased countrywide.

Lech Walesa addresses striking workers on February 3, 1981, in Bielsko Biala.

The democratic Western world thought that if the Polish Communist government could be destabilized, the collapse of Soviet dominance in Eastern Europe would be hastened. The key to this was Solidarity. The Vatican and the United States supported Solidarity financially and with communication equipment, such as printing presses, shortwave radios, fax machines, and computers.

Solidarity intercepted national radio and television programming with resistance messages, ending Communist control of the mass media. In one such interception, at a national soccer championship, a banner with the

"The world reacted with silence or with mere sympathy when Polish frontiers were crossed by invading armies and the sovereign state has to succumb to brutal force. Our national history has so often filled us with bitterness and the feeling of helplessness."
—Lech Walesa, in his acceptance speech for the Nobel Peace Prize in 1983

words "Solidarity lives!" appeared on screen at halftime, and a message was broadcast calling for resistance.

In June 1983 John Paul II visited Poland, his second visit to his homeland after being elected pope in 1978. In July the Military Council for National Salvation, led by Jaruzelski, was dissolved; the following year thousands of political prisoners were released. In 1988 Solidarity led worker strikes across the country demanding political dialogue. Weeks of negotiation among the government, the union, and the Church led to a historic accord in 1989 that legally reinstated Solidarity and paved the way for opposition politics and free elections. The state media monopoly was lifted, and a new constitution was adopted.

THE IRON CURTAIN FALLS

In 1989 Poles voted in their first free elections in more than forty years. Solidarity won all the Sejm seats that it was entitled to contest and all but one of the Senate seats. A coalition government was formed, with Tadeusz Mazowiecki as prime minister and Jaruzelski as president. But the new government faced the old economic problems: serious under-investment and poor industry and productivity. Foreign investment was sought, a stock exchange opened, and the Polish currency devalued.

In 1990 Jaruzelski stepped down, and Walesa won the presidential election. The new government elected Jan Bielecki as prime minister. But after years of one-party rule, Poland's new political problem was having too many parties, none of which were strong enough to govern alone. Successive ministers tried in vain to gain enough support from the different parties in the Sejm to form a strong base for governing. In 1993 Walesa decided to dissolve the fragmented Sejm.

The party that seemed to answer most Poles' political desires was the Democratic Left Alliance, led by Aleksander Kwasniewski, a former Communist. Kwasniewski beat Walesa in the 1995 presidential election, and in 2000 he was re-elected.

In 1999 Poland joined NATO. The North Atlantic Treaty Organization (NATO) is a political and military alliance of twenty-eight member nations

LECH WALESA

Lech Walesa was born in 1943. He was a spirited student and loved to argue with his teachers. He hated farming and wanted to be an engineer, but his parents could not afford to send him to college. Walesa took a part-time job while attending courses at a trade school. During his military service, he was recommended for promotion, but Walesa did not choose to become a military leader.

Already known as a skilled worker, in 1967 he found a job at the gigantic Lenin Shipyards in Gdansk. At work he laid electric cables in fishing boats; at home, in a cramped house shared with three other workers, he listened to Radio Free Europe and talked politics.

With the economy worsening, shipyard workers got less time to do a job and no extra pay. Productivity did not increase, and in 1970 new price increases were announced. Strikes erupted all along the Baltic coast, and Walesa was at the head of a column of protesters. From then on, his life was filled with speeches to fellow workers and reasoned, if heated, arguments with his employers, and later with government representatives. When a worker with thirty years' service at the shipyard was fired in 1980 for distributing political pamphlets, general indignation sparked a strike demanding a free labor union, free speech, and the right to strike. Feeling strongly that God was on their side, Walesa negotiated a successful settlement, and Solidarity was born.

More years of political turmoil followed. Walesa was spurned, praised, arrested, imprisoned—until in 1983 he was awarded the Nobel Peace Prize for his efforts. That brought added international prestige. He led negotiations in 1989 that resulted in Poland's first non-Communist government in forty years. By that time, Walesa and his family were living in a large villa in Gdansk. Polish workers cheered him still but saw that he was dressed better than they were, getting a little fat, and suffering from back problems. He was tired and told them, "You have to create a couple of new Walesas. I did my part." But fate had yet another part in store for him. In 1990, nine years after he and his movement had been banned, Walesa became the president of Poland.

In 1995, Walesa founded the Lech Walesa Institute to protect Polish independence and strengthen its democracy and free-market economics. Walesa has written several books and remains active in European and global social and political life.

Polish President Aleksander Kwasniewski addresses **NATO** in 1999.

(as of 2015), including Canada and the United States. This membership signaled a huge change for Poland, as NATO membership ensures security against outside forces, such as the increasingly powerful Russia, which invaded Romania's neighbor Ukraine in 2014. (Ukraine was not a NATO member.)

In 2003 members of the Polish government supported the US invasion of Iraq, and Poland sent two thousand troops to be part of a multinational stabilization force in south-central Iraq. In 2004, along with nine other nations, Poland joined the European Union (EU) and began the difficult transition from a centrally controlled economy to a more free-market system. The EU is an economic and political partnership between twenty-eight (as of 2015) European nations. It was created in the aftermath of WWII to foster a sense of interdependence and unity among European nations in order to deter future conflicts. In order to be a part of the EU, a member state must abide by its standards for human rights, freedoms, democracy, and equality.

BROTHERS IN CHARGE

In 2005, Lech Kaczynski of the conservative Law and Justice Party became the president of Poland. He had been the mayor of Warsaw for the three years before that. During his time in office, he worked to improve relations with the United States. He also pledged to pursue justice against those who were responsible for the Communist crimes of the past. During his administration, charges were brought against the former Communist leader General Wojciech Jaruzelski for his role in enforcing martial law in 1981 during the time of the Solidarity uprisings.

Curiously, Kaczynski had an identical twin brother, Jaroslaw, who was also active in political affairs. In 2006, Jaroslaw became prime minister of Poland while Lech was the president. In 2010, en route to a commemorative ceremony for the Polish victims of a 1940 massacre at the hands of the

Soviet secret police, Lech Kaczynski died in a plane crash that also killed many other high officials in the Polish government. Jaroslaw was not among them. When elections were held for a new president, Jaroslaw Kacyzski ran, offering to fill his brother's place, but he lost the election to the Parliament Speaker and Acting President Bronisław Komorowski.

Polish President Lech Kaczynski, left, congratulates his identical twin brother Jaroslaw Kaczynski, right, just after nominating him to be the new Polish Prime Minister in 2006.

INTERNET LINKS

abel.hive.no/trumpet/articles/hejnal/hejnal.mp3
Listen to the Hejnal trumpet call.

www.lonelyplanet.com/poland/history#pageTitle
This tourism site presents a good overview of Poland's history.

news.bbc.co.uk/2/hi/europe/country_profiles/1054724.stm
BBC News "Poland timeline" offers a chronology of events dating from 966 CE.

www.nobelprize.org/nobel_prizes/peace/laureates/1983/walesa-lecture.html
The official site of the Nobel Prize offers the text of Lech Walesa's acceptance speech in 1983.

www.history.com/topics/american-revolution/tadeusz-kosciuszko
This site presents a good article about Tadeusz Kosciuszko.

GOVERNMENT

The flag of Poland, perched atop the famous Sigimund's Column in Warsaw, flies against a stormy sky.

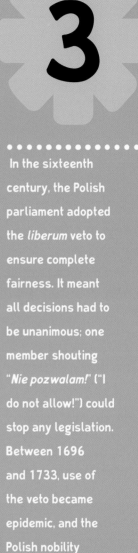

3

HAVING REGARD FOR THE EXISTENCE and future of our Homeland, which recovered, in 1989, the possibility of a sovereign and democratic determination of its fate, we, the Polish Nation ... Beholden to our ancestors for their labors, their struggle for independence achieved at great sacrifice ... Obliged to bequeath to future generations all that is valuable from our over one thousand years' heritage ... Desiring to guarantee the rights of the citizens for all time ... Hereby establish this Constitution of the Republic of Poland as the basic law for the State ...

So begins (here in abridged form) the Polish Constitution, as established in 1997. The document goes on to say that Poland is a democratic state ruled by law, which upholds social justice, safeguards the independence and integrity of its territory, ensures the freedoms, rights, and security of its citizens, and protects the national heritage.

In the sixteenth century, the Polish parliament adopted the *liberum* veto to ensure complete fairness. It meant all decisions had to be unanimous; one member shouting *"Nie pozwalam!"* ("I do not allow!") could stop any legislation. Between 1696 and 1733, use of the veto became epidemic, and the Polish nobility agreed on nothing.

THE FIRST CONSTITUTION

Poland was the first country in Europe to have a constitution. The United States adopted its constitution only four years earlier. Poland's Constitution Day, May 3, 1791, is an annual holiday.

Poland's constitution introduced the concept of the sovereignty of a people, including the middle classes as well as the nobility. Political and judicial power was separated. Government was delegated to a cabinet responsible to the *Sejm* (saym). Cities were allowed self-determination, and the peasants gained legal protection. The constitution, which was considered progressive for its time, was in force a mere nineteen months. It was abolished in 1793 after Russia invaded Poland.

The memory of that constitution, however, kept hope alive among the Poles for a future independent, just society.

Poland's new constitution guarantees all its citizens basic rights that are common to most European and North American constitutions and that conform to the European Convention on Human Rights. The constitution also spells out the role of local government and of nongovernmental organizations in the process of forming stable democratic institutions. Voting

From 1952 to 1989, the country's name was the People's Republic of Poland. Following that momentous year—1989—it became the Republic of Poland. Though the names seem to mean the same thing, they don't. A "People's Republic" has come to be a term associated with Communist governments, though there are one or two exceptions. A Republic, on the other hand, is a form of government which is ruled by elected officials and run according to law. In many cases, that law is in the form of a Constitution.

After the fall of the Soviet Union, and with it the demise of Communism in the Eastern Bloc, Poland became a parliamentary republic. That is one in which the head of state and the head of government are two different positions: the head of state is the president and the head of government is the prime minister. Typically the prime minister has more power. Many European nations have adopted this form of government. (The United States, by contrast, is a presidential republic, one in which the head of state and the head of government are one and the same, embodied in the president.)

age is eighteen and suffrage is universal, meaning that all citizens eighteen and over can vote.

Poland's constitution established a government with three branches: executive, legislative, and judiciary.

EXECUTIVE Power is shared by the president of the country and the cabinet, or Council of Ministers. The president is the head of state and the supreme commander of the armed forces. He or she is elected to a five-year term and works closely with the prime minister, who heads the council. The president has the duty to ensure the nation's commitment to its own constitution and to international treaties, and the power to call for parliamentary elections and to propose or veto legislation.

The main work of running the government and writing laws is the responsibility of the Council of Ministers and their leader. The prime minister is appointed by the president and approved by the Sejm, the lower house of parliament. He or she is therefore usually a member of the party that controls the majority of seats in the Sejm.

The National
Assembly meets in
June 2014.

LEGISLATIVE The legislature is a bi-cameral, or two house, national assembly. Its power is shared by two independent elected bodies: the *Sejm* (Saym) and the Senate. The 460-seat Sejm is the main house, with most of the authority to debate and pass laws. Members are elected according to proportional representation every four years.

Members of both the Sejm and the 100-seat Senate serve four-year terms. The Senate, with fewer powers than the Sejm, functions in a supervisory and advisory role. The Senate can comment on and amend laws written by the Sejm, but the Sejm can override the Senate's decisions with a simple majority vote.

JUDICIAL Legal authority is split among three offices—the Supreme Court, the Constitutional Tribunal, and the State Tribunal.

The Supreme Court is the highest court and the court of last appeal. It has more than one hundred judges, recommended by the National Judicial

Council, which consists of twenty-four judges serving four-year terms, and appointed by the country's president. They serve for an indefinite period. The Sejm appoints the first president of the Supreme Court on the recommendation of the country's president.

The Supreme Court, with its four chambers (civil; criminal; labor, social security, and public affairs; and military), supervises the common, military, and administrative courts, and is the court of appeal against judgments made in the lower courts.

The Constitutional Tribunal has fifteen judges, selected by the Sejm for nine-year terms. They make judgments on the constitutionality of laws and their execution by government bodies.

The State Tribunal rules on constitutional or legal infringements by officials holding the highest positions in government. It has the power to remove officials from public office and to prevent candidates from holding office or voting.

The President of the Republic of Poland, (2010-), Bronisław Komorowski

INTERNET LINKS

www.president.pl/en
President.pl is the official site of the President of the Republic of Poland. It is excellent, informative, and in English.

www.cia.gov/library/publications/resources/the-world-factbook/geos/pl.html
CIA World Factbook: Poland, Government page explains the basic structure of the Polish government and lists current office holders.

ECONOMY

A ten-year-old Polish boy celebrates Poland's accession to the European Union in 2004.

4

POLAND HAS GONE THROUGH AN amazing transformation in a very short time. In less than three decades, the country has moved from a Communist economic system to a free market economy. Not only has Poland succeeded in accomplishing such an about-face, but it has seen its economy grow at a rate of more than four percent per year, faster than any other economy in Europe. It has also managed to attract a great deal of foreign investment in its companies and infrastructure.

Poland's economy received a big boost when the country became a member of the European Union (EU) in 2004. Historically, Poland had looked to the East, politically and economically. By joining the EU, however, Poland firmly announced itself as a Western nation. In order to be a part of the EU, a member state must abide by its standards for human rights, freedoms, democracy, and equality.

McDonald's opened its first restaurant in Poland in 1992, three years after the collapse of communism. In 2014, it had 338 branches in Poland, and was the leading fast food chain.

TIES WITH GERMANY

As a result of their EU associations, Germany and Poland are now important economic partners. Both countries benefit from the relationship. Germany buys about 25 percent of Poland's exports, and Poland imports about 25 percent of its goods from Germany. Poland also serves as a production base for some German companies. It offers highly skilled but lower cost labor because Polish salaries remain lower, on average, than those in most Western European countries. In return, Polish factories get business that might otherwise go to other countries. Many German industries are able to produce goods in Poland for less than what they would cost to make in China. Poland's next-door proximity to Germany cuts transportation costs that production in Asian factories would require.

In the Polish city of Poznan, for example, a Volkswagen factory employs 6,900 workers who produce 155,000 vehicles each year. Similarly, a United Kingdom company employs four thousand workers in Poland who build heavy trucks, city buses, and bus chassis at three different factories. In fact, automobiles and automotive components are Poland's leading export, which is notable considering Poland doesn't have an internationally known car brand of its own.

Workers inspect an Opel Astra automobile at General Motors' Adam Opel AG manufacturing plant in Gliwice, Poland, in 2014.

IMPROVED INFRASTRUCTURE

One of the problems holding Poland back from economic development was its transportation infrastructure. Its highways were old, narrow, overcrowded, and insufficient, and its train stations and rails were crumbling. If a country can't quickly and efficiently get its goods transported from factory to market, or even get its people from one place to another, its economy will remain bogged down. Between 2000 and 2013, the EU invested nearly 40 billion euros ($45.6 billion) in Polish infrastructure.

Although more improvement remains, new highways and renovated railroads have already dramatically reduced the cost and the time it takes to transport goods to the West. Broadband internet services, necessary for any business, have greatly expanded. And continuing through 2020, the EU plans to help Poland with another €106 billion ($120.9 billion).

MINING

Hard coal is abundant in Poland, especially in the Upper Silesian region; its vast coal reserves are the second largest in Europe, and supply 90 percent of the country's energy needs. However, the Polish coal industry has been the focus of restructuring and privatization efforts since the 1990s. Many of its coal mines have been closed down because they were inefficient and unprofitable. Moreover, environmental concerns have caused friction between Poland and its EU partners, who are pressuring Poland to cut its carbon emissions.

The inefficiency of Poland's mines means the coal cannot compete on the international market against less expensive sources. Even some Polish people themselves have taken to buying cheaper Russian coal, which only exacerbates this volatile situation.

INDUSTRY

Poland manufactures steel, chemicals, glass, paper, washing machines, refrigerators, televisions, and motor vehicles, among other products. When many of its industrial areas were set up, more than half the output went to the Soviet Union or other Communist countries. Now most Polish exports go to countries in the European Union and Southeast Asia.

The old royal city of Krakow stands about 40 miles (64 km) east of the main mining area. Wroclaw, on the Oder River, is an important industrial center about 90 miles (144.8 km) to the north-northwest. Lodz is the center of Poland's textile industry. Cottons, woolens, silks, and linens are made there. Poland was, for some time, Europe's largest producer of flax and has a significant linen industry.

A worker stands on a raised platform to harvest tomatoes from the top of the vines at a wholesale vegetable production plant operated by Citronex Group in Siechnice, Poland.

AGRICULTURE

EU membership has helped the agriculture sector as well. When Poland transitioned from communism, it had some two million small farms. Many produced only enough food for their own needs using old fashioned technology such as horse-drawn machinery. Today, although half of the existing farms are still household subsistence plots, others have benefitted from EU investment and increased spending from the Polish government.

The dairy sector, for example, had to modernize in order to meet EU standards, and that paid off by attracting international agri-food companies to Poland. This, in turn, increased food exports and cut down on the amount of food products that Poland needs to import.

All in all, this is a healthy economic situation to be in. Poland exports processed fruit and vegetables, meat, and dairy products. It is the top EU producer of potatoes and rye, and one of the world's leading producers of sugar beets and triticale.

Polish farms also raise cattle, sheep, and hogs. In recent years, Poland has even surpassed China to become the world's largest producer and exporter of apples.

SHOPPING

During the forty years of Communist control, Poles stood in long lines to buy the most basic products, such as food and clothes. Shopping could take all day. The expression *niema* (NYE-ma), meaning "there is none," became almost a joke.

Today Poles can find all the goods they could want in shops and markets, although not everyone might be able to afford them. Shopping malls are being built on the outskirts of larger cities. Major European brands are now

SHIPBUILDING

Many of Poland's shipyards were destroyed in World War II, and it was not until 1949 that Poland's first postwar ocean-going vessel was launched. Under state control, Poland's shipbuilding industry changed from steam to diesel power.

In the 1970s, the yards were modified with new technology. The Lenin Shipyards in Gdansk could boast a steady output of factory ships from fishing vessels and ferries to container and bulk-cargo carriers. In the 1980s, the industry included six shipyards, twenty-one equipment factories, and three research and development centers, altogether employing about fifty-seven thousand people. At that time, Poland exported most of its products to the Soviet Union. Some one thousand plants across the country supplied materials to the shipbuilding industry.

At the start of the twenty-first century, however, the shipbuilding industry was plagued with corruption and fiscal mismanagement, and in 2009, the industry all but collapsed. The Gdynia and Szczecin shipyards were sold to an unnamed private investor, but when the investor did not pay up, the shipyards went into bankruptcy.

available to urbanites in Poland. There are also hypermarkets on the outskirts of Warsaw and in many other major cities.

For bargain hunters, the best places to go are the bazaars. In Warsaw, hundreds of petty traders "set up shop" on weekends in front of the huge department store buildings, in the shadow of the Palace of Culture and Science. The largest bazaar is in the former national stadium in the capital city's eastern Praga district. The bazaars sell clocks, watches, antique furniture, paintings, and everyday items such as toys, clothes and shoes, fruit and vegetables.

The bazaars are a vital source of extra income not only for Poles but also people from neighboring countries. Whether this is smuggling or

Poland has enjoyed strong economic growth since joining the EU in 2004. Now it must decide when to adopt the euro as its currency. One of the conditions of joining the EU is that the country is obliged to give up its traditional unit of money—in this case, the zloty—and switch to the euro, the common currency of the EU. However, with no firm timetable in place for such a swap, Poland appears to be taking its time.

EU countries that use the euro are part of what is called the eurozone. At the moment, Poland's Constitution prevents such a move—it declares the zloty the national currency—and will have to be amended first. Such a change will require a two-thirds majority vote in Parliament, and in recent years, most Poles have opposed adopting the euro.

Nevertheless, some financial analysts say the country would benefit from making the change. They say it would anchor Poland more securely in Western institutions and increase its political clout.

Another hurdle to entering the eurozone is that the EU member country must meet certain economic criteria before joining. As of April 2014, Poland met three of the five criteria.

Meanwhile, public opinion may be changing. The 2014 Russian military intervention in Ukraine caused some euro objectors to reconsider, and the topic became a subject of debate prior to the parliamentary elections of 2015. Most observers doubt the currency will switch before 2019.

"trade tourism" depends on one's point of view. The practice began in 1989 when Poles, allowed into West Berlin, flooded in with vodka at half the usual price, found ready customers, and loaded up with goods to sell back home. Russians used to flock to these bazaars to find bargains, but can now get similar goods at home. Warsaw's old-style bazaars are declining, but still remain popular among traders and tourists.

Warsaw, the capital of Poland, is sometimes called "the phoenix city" because of the way it arose from the ashes of World War II like the mythical bird. Poland's economic success has many people wondering just how high this phoenix will fly. Some economic projections suggest that Poland's economy will grow by about 2.5 percent per year through 2030. That would make it one of the top twenty economies in the world. Can Poland do it? For investors and economists, as well as for the everyday Polish citizen, it's an intriguing question.

INTERNET LINKS

www.numbeo.com/cost-of-living/country_result.jsp?country=Poland
This site lists the average price of consumer goods in Poland and the equivalent in US dollars.

www.economywatch.com/economic-statistics/country/Poland
Economy Watch has a large number of economic statistics for Poland.

www.bloomberg.com/bw/articles/2013-11-27/how-poland-became-europes-most-dynamic-economy
"How Poland Became Europe's Most Dynamic Economy" is a 2013 article on Bloomberg.

www.foreignaffairs.com/articles/140336/mitchell-a-orenstein/six-markets-to-watch-poland
Foreign Affairs offers "Six Markets to Watch: Poland," an excellent article about Poland's economic rise.

ENVIRONMENT

A stork stands on a rooftop nest in the village of Zywkowo in northern Poland.

5

JUST AS THE ECONOMY IN Poland has improved, so has the environment. Decades of Communist rule left deep scars—the Communist authorities made decisions based on political and economic factors and had very little concern for the environment.

The situation in post-Communist Poland is definitely improving, but that doesn't mean all problems have been solved. The barriers to environmental conservation initiatives remain economic. Logging, for instance, threatens the survival of the 84 percent of the Bialowieza Forest that lies outside the Bialowieza National Park. Activists have since 1994 been campaigning for the enlargement of the national park, which protects only a small section of the forest. But theirs is a mammoth task, since logging remains one of the few profitable industries in a region of high unemployment. Also, the local people there are long accustomed to heating their homes with the wood from the forest and consider that lifestyle a right.

As transportation networks penetrate previously inaccessible areas, modern highways will connect Poland to Western Europe. But such development will divide virgin forests and push wildlife into ever-shrinking refuges.

Now that Poland is a part of the European Union, laws and regulations need to be formulated and refined to protect the country's fragile ecosystems from a surge of urbanization and industrial development. Manufacturing plants have to upgrade their facilities and equipment in order to reduce the amount of harmful substances they release

Each spring, about fifty thousand white storks, or about 20 percent of the world's population, leave their wintering grounds in Africa and flock to Poland to nest. Many storks build large nests on rooftops. Fortunately, in Poland this is considered good luck. A Polish saying goes, "If a stork builds a nest on your roof, you will have a happy family life."

Enviromentalists
from international
organizations
protest the 2013
Coal and Climate
Summit taking
place in the Polish
Ministry of
Economy in
Warsaw.

into the air and waterways. Funds from the European Union finance the building of community infrastructure and waste-disposal facilities to support Poland in cleaning up its natural environment.

AIR POLLUTION

One of the most noticeable improvements after the fall of communism was the drop in air pollution. Many outdated factories closed down, which immediately caused a drop in emissions, particularly of sulphur dioxide and nitrous oxide. As new industries slowly opened, the emissions did not increase because the modern facilities use more environmentally friendly technologies. Likewise, the energy and transportation sectors modernized, which has helped reduce the concentration of airborne pollutants. Although more Poles own cars now than in the past, the newer vehicles meet the EU standards and are far less polluting.

Despite all that good news, however, Poland still has some of the dirtiest air in Europe. A 2013 study by the European Environment Agency (EEA) found that Poland had the second worst air pollution in Europe, exceeded only by Bulgaria. In 2011, six of the top ten most polluted cities in Europe were in Poland. In addition, the country had the highest levels of benzo(a)pyrene, a carcinogenic hydrocarbon that's found in coal tar and also comes from wood burning and car exhaust. BaP is a growing problem in Europe, especially in areas where domestic coal and wood burning is common, as it is in Poland.

Poland's abundant reserves of brown coal are its main source of fuel, generating 90 percent of its electricity. Brown coal is also burned to supply towns and cities with heat during the winter months. Travelers to Poland are often warned about the poor air quality in the country during winter.

While the EU pushes all members to adopt clean, renewable energy sources like wind and solar, Poland is clinging to coal, claiming it cannot afford to switch. Coal mining plays too important a role in the economy to give it up, government officials say. The largest coal-fired utility plant in all of Europe is in Belchatow, Poland. That plant is also Europe's largest carbon emitter.

Air pollution, of course, is more than a problem of smoggy scenery; it's a dangerous health issue. It is linked to a number of health conditions, including low birth weight in babies, asthma, heart disease, and kidney damage. The airborne particulate matter from burning coal has been found to cause lung cancer.

WATER POLLUTION

Despite having so many rivers, many communities in Poland lack clean water due to the poor planning of the Communist government. Because of the high cost associated with equipping existing communities with sewage treatment facilities, the current government has been slow in addressing water pollution in the country.

For example, in 2013, the European Commission took Poland to the EU Court of Justice for failing to adequately address the problem of water pollution by nitrates. Nitrates are essential for plants to grow, and they are widely used as fertilizers, but excess levels cause severe water pollution. Farm runoff pollutes groundwater as well as rivers and lakes. And because most of Poland's rivers flow into the Baltic Sea, pollutants end up there as well. Excess levels of nitrates can damage both fresh water and the marine environment by causing an excessive growth of algae that chokes out other life. This process is called eutrophication. Drinking water supplies also

The European, or Eurasian, beaver was hunted to near extinction a century ago. After major flooding in Poland in 2010, government authorities determined that the beavers were responsible for causing the flooding and demanded the culling of the animals.

suffer from excess nitrates and the process of purifying them is expensive. The EU actions were intended to prod the Polish government to step up its plans for addressing and correcting the problems.

EUROPE'S NATURAL HISTORY

Some of Poland's rare animals are struggling to survive as human activity shrinks their natural habitat. Poland's national parks protect the country's endangered species. The oldest of the parks is part of the Bialowieza Forest, the last section of a primeval forest that covered most of Europe's lowlands thousands of years ago. The forest extends across the border into Belarus, making it one of the most important natural refuges in Europe. It shelters one of Europe's most precious animals—the European bison. Poaching and hunting decimated many bison populations in the 1800s. The biggest free-range herbivore in Europe, the bison eats ferns, lichens, mosses, and the bark and leaves of trees. It can grow to more than 1,700 pounds (770 kg) in weight. Bulls tend to live alone, except during the mating season. The European bison was gradually reintroduced in the wild in the 1900s. Today, most live in the Bialowieza Forest.

The Tatra National Park has as its symbol the chamois, also protected under Polish law. The Bialowieza, Kampinos, and Tatra National Parks are all UNESCO biosphere reserves. They are conservation areas that support sustainable development as well as international sharing of environmental research findings. The European lynx, for a while absent from its historical habitat in the Polish lowlands, has been reintroduced in Poland, particularly in the Kampinos National Park, where it lives as a protected species. Elk and European beaver are two other mammals that have been successfully reintroduced in Kampinos.

The Baltic Sea is home to the harbor porpoise, whose numbers have decreased drastically due largely to accidental capture in fishing nets. The porpoise is a mammal like the whale and dolphin but is smaller and has no beak. The harbor porpoise rises to breathe every few minutes when feeding. It eats fish and can weigh up to 145 pounds (65 kg).

Poland works with other signatories to the Agreement on the Conservation of Small Cetaceans of the Baltic and North Seas, to strengthen international law on the killing of such animals, to monitor their population and food supply, to reduce pollution in the seas, and to improve fishing practices.

INTERNET LINKS

www.eea.europa.eu/soer/countries/pl
The European Environment Agency country profile of Poland has information about pollution and other challenges.

www.theguardian.com/environment/gallery/2011/apr/06/bialowieza-europe-forest-in-pictures
An image gallery from *The Guardian* has impressive pictures of Poland's Bialowieza Forest.

www.theguardian.com/world/2011/apr/06/poland-environmentalists-foresters-primeval-forest
"Poland's environmentalists fight foresters for heart of primeval forest" discusses the environmental conflicts between ecologists, foresters, and loggers.

wwf.panda.org/who_we_are/wwf_offices/poland
This site offers several articles on WWF conservation projects in Poland as well as environmental news.

wwf.panda.org/how_you_can_help/live_green/travel/on_vacation/eco_tips/poland
The WWF Eco-Tips page offers a quick overview of the environmental situation in Poland.

THE POLES

A couple dressed in traditional clothing dances at a festival in Krakow.

6

POLAND TODAY IS THE MOST homogeneous state in Europe. The Polish people are almost all Slavs and speak the same language with some regional differences. And the majority are Roman Catholics.

Their Slavic heritage gives the Poles generally light-colored hair and eyes and a slightly dark complexion. However, intermarriages that occurred during the nation's history of foreign invasions have resulted in a population with diverse physical characteristics.

In 2010, children celebrate the two hundredth birthday of Frederic Chopin with traditional folk dances in Warsaw.

Some twenty million people of Polish descent live outside of Poland, making it one of the largest diasporas in the world, and one of the most widely dispersed. About ten million Americans are of Polish descent, and one of the largest Polish American communities is in Chicago.

Polish soccer fans cheer for the home team during a qualifying match against Germany for the UEFA EURO 2016.

Border movements in the past displaced Germans, Ukrainians, Belarusians, and Lithuanians living near Poland's borders. These peoples established minority communities that today, along with other, smaller minority groups, make up less than 5 percent of the population. Jews number around eight thousand, mostly in Warsaw. Before World War II, Poland was home to Europe's largest Jewish community—more than three million people.

On the other hand, there are Poles living in Ukraine, Belarus, and Lithuania. Poles who were forced to leave their homeland for political or economic reasons include the thousands who, during World War II, lost their lands and were sent to Kazakhstan and Siberia, where they were forbidden to speak Polish or talk about what had happened to them. Yet other Poles left on their own will, settling in the United States, Canada, and Western European countries.

MINORITY GROUPS

Magyar horsemen swept through Poland in the ninth century. Mongol horsemen invaded in the thirteenth century. The Polish king subsequently opened his country to outsiders if they would come and repopulate its devastated lands. Millions came, including Jews fleeing persecution in other parts of Europe. Fifteenth- and sixteenth-century Poland was a country of religious tolerance. There were nearly a hundred mosques in the country and most towns had a synagogue. Shifting borders through the centuries resulted in small pockets of ethnic minorities being left inside or outside Poland. When from 1919 to 1921 the borders of the Second Republic were drawn, Poland was the sixth largest territory in Europe, with ethnic minorities totalling some nine million—about a third of the population.

A Slav teen wears a blouse of traditional Ukrainian design.

UKRAINIANS When the borders changed yet again in 1945, there were some 700,000 Ukrainians living in Poland. Some moved reluctantly to what became the Ukrainian Soviet Socialist Republic. Most fought for the right to stay. By 1947 the Polish authorities decided to send the remaining 200,000 Ukrainians elsewhere. Most were sent to the west, where there were empty farms left by the Germans, but no more than two or three Ukrainian families were ever allowed to settle in the same village.

According to the 2011 Polish census, there are about fifty-one thousand Ukrainians remaining. Deliberately separated by the Communists, the Polish Ukrainians struggle to maintain their traditions. The Festival of Ukrainian Culture at Sopot, where choirs and dance groups celebrate with true Ukrainian music, is held every other year.

However, recent events in neighboring Ukraine have changed things. In 2014, the eruption of violence by Russian separatists and the related Russian annexation of the Crimea resulted in a marked uptick in Ukrainians seeking to move to Poland. Some sought refugee status; according to the Polish government agency dealing with immigration matters, Poland received 2,318 asylum petitions from Ukrainians in 2014 compared to forty-six the year before. In addition, in 2015, Poland planned to offer eleven thousand work permits to Ukrainian nationals, a 30 percent increase over the previous year.

BELARUSIANS Around forty-seven thousand Belarusians live in the east of Poland, mostly around the Bialystok area. Near Siemiatycze is the Holy Mount of Grabarka, where Belarusian pilgrims, of the old Orthodox Church, climb carrying crosses to the summit. A Belarusian Democratic Union was founded in 1990 to represent the interests of Poland's Belarusian community.

LITHUANIANS Around eight thousand Lithuanians live in the Punsk area near the Polish border with Lithuania. Punsk has the only Lithuanian school in Poland. It is also where Poland's Lithuanian community runs a few societies and centers to promote their culture and language and tighten the bonds among the members of their community.

GERMANS In the 2011 census, about 148,000 residents claimed German ethnicity. Most live in the Silesia region, which borders Germany and the Czech Republic. The Potsdam Conference of 1945 approved the repatriation of Germans, who were replaced by Poles returning home from exile or imprisonment in the Soviet Union and other countries. So people in the west and southwest of Poland are not all descended from original Polish inhabitants. Many are of pure German ancestry.

POLISH JEWS

The first Jews to settle in Poland probably came from beyond the Volga River, an area that had established Judaism as a state religion in the eighth century. When Jews were expelled from other European countries in the Middle Ages, they were accepted in Poland. They were allowed to cultivate their culture and customs. In 1939 there were about 3.5 million Jews in Poland—about 10 percent of the country's population. They were doctors, teachers, scientists, industrialists, bankers, and businessmen. When the Nazis occupied Poland during WWII, they killed about 90 percent of those people.

Today there are thought to be about twenty thousand people at most with Jewish roots left in Poland. Of those who survived the Holocaust, thousands emigrated to Israel or the United States. Others simply left Judaism. For the sake of survival during the war, some Jews became practicing Catholics and assimilated into the Polish Catholic population. For their children and grandchildren, many of whom were never told the family's secret, discovering the truth about their ancestry can come as a shock. Some revert to Judaism.

THE GORALE, PEOPLE OF THE HIGHLANDS

Not a minority group but an identity group, Polish highlanders known as the Gorale (goor-AH-le), or the Gorals, are an independent-minded people with a distinctive mountain way of life. The Gorale live in the Podhale region in the Tatra Mountains. Traditionally pastoralists, they raise sheep and goats, growing only a few crops, such as oats, barley, or potatoes.

With access to more modern agricultural methods today, the Gorale have ventured into dairy farming. The men do the work that involves the use of horses, machines, and tools such as scythes, while the women and children rake, turn hay, plant and gather potatoes, and weed the vegetables.

Most Gorale live in small villages of wooden houses surrounded by long strip fields, pastures, and forest. There is a growing tendency for young couples to establish a new household, but the three-generation extended family is still common. Two-room wooden huts stand beside modern multi-story brick houses. But even in the modern houses, families tend to live, eat, and sleep in one or two rooms while renting the other rooms to tourists.

The Podhale has several market towns and a few resorts. One of the poorest areas in Poland, it is now benefiting from the tourist dollar.

The Gorale are strongly and uniformly Catholic. For them, religious events are the most important annual events. They wear traditional clothes to Mass and to church processions. Women show off lace-trimmed aprons over colorful skirts with embroidered "waistcoat" tops, and black, gold-trimmed caps. Men wear white felt pants with a striped design at the side, and broad belts, sometimes sashes, and black-rimmed hats. The shepherds carry traditional axe-like crooks, which are necessary for rescuing stray lambs on the mountainside.

Every Easter, Christmas, and May (the month devotions to the Virgin Mary are celebrated), the churches and shrines are beautifully decorated. The old lifestyle has persisted despite years under Austrian rule, Nazi invasion, and Communist rule.

Nevertheless, the Jewish community in Poland is slowly coming back to life. Krakow, for example, hosts a large annual Jewish festival that attracts thousands of international visitors. And in 2014, the new Museum of the History of Polish Jews opened in Warsaw.

TRADITIONAL COSTUMES

In fourteenth-century Poland, only nobility had the right to wear red. That was how the word *karmazyn* (kar-MA-zyn), or "crimson," came to mean gentleman. Poles today often wear clothes of predominantly red and white, because those are the national colors of Poland.

The *kontousch* (kon-TUSH), an overgarment with slashed sleeve, and its *joupane* (yo-PA-ne), the undergarment of a long tunic, show the influence of the Asiatic world. The style was probably copied from Persia—Poland's borders once stretched to the Black Sea. Similarly, the baggy pants and flowing cloaks of the men could have Turkish origins. Polish men traditionally

A young girl wears a traditional Lowicz costume during a Corpus Christi procession in Lowicz, Poland.

wore fur caps. Peasants wore short tunics of hand-woven materials in soft natural colors. They also wore long pants, a cloak of sheepskin, and boots or shoes made from woven strips of bark.

The important element is decoration: edgings in brightly contrasting materials, trimmings of colored string, red or green lapels on coats, studded belts, metal ornaments, appliqué work, and embroidery. The richest appliqué work can be seen on the leather bodices and pants in the Carpathian mountain area. Lace and crochet are made in intricate designs, especially in Silesia.

Polish women delight in wearing amber bead necklaces. This was a way for a prospective bride to show off her wealth. Amber from the Baltic is increasingly precious, especially if there is a fossilized insect trapped in the resin. Coral beads are thought to bring good luck, in the form of many healthy children. Today, however, such finery is reserved for Sunday dress or special festivals. On those days, women wear red and blue pleated skirts, with a richly floral blouse and, for older women, a headscarf. For the rest of the week, they wear more somber or casual clothes, such as black skirts, dark suits, or T-shirts and jeans.

Another aspect of Polish tradition is their love of horses. Horses were a symbol of warrior status. They were lovingly cared for, covered in rich cloths at parades, adorned with plumes, and dyed on special occasions. The favorite color was red, but for funerals, black with a purple or green mane and tail was a popular combination. Turkish horses were crossed with European breeds, and the Polish cavalry outnumbered the infantry three to one in the seventeenth century.

INTERNET LINKS

www.staypoland.com/famous-poles.htm
This site presents short descriptions of famous Poles in various categories.

www.mypolishtimes.com/index.php/articles/1222-gorale-proud-highlanders-not-hillbillies-36-2013
"Gorale—proud highlanders, not hillbillies" discusses the culture of the Polish Gorale people.

www.perfekt.krakow.pl/en
This manufacturer and distributor of Polish regional costumes displays many folk styles according to various regions, a map of those regions, and photos of folk festivals.

www.theguardian.com/commentisfree/2014/nov/01/polish-jewish-relations-warsaw-museum-history-polish-jews
"A small miracle in the tortured history of Polish-Jewish relations" is a moving article about the opening of the Jewish museum in Warsaw and reflections on Jewish life in Poland.

7

Compared to people in the other European Union countries, Poles marry at the youngest age: 25.6 years old for women and 27.5 years old for men, on average (2010).

I T IS DIFFICULT, IF NOT FOOLHARDY, TO try to sum up national characteristics, but robust patriotism is surely the keynote to Polish character. Few can deny that Polish determination and cheerfulness have been unshakeable in the face of hardship. This has resulted in a rowdy, friendly public life. During the martial law years, when protest could lead to imprisonment, many Poles wore buttons printed with "DOWN WITH THE MILITARY JUNTA" in large letters, followed in tiny letters by "in El Salvador." It was not a very significant protest, but it was typical of the Poles' refusal to admit defeat. After the secret police were removed in 1956, freedom of speech blossomed.

The wry humor of the Polish people is illustrated in the way residents will explain to visitors that the best view of the city of Warsaw is from the top of the thirty-seven-story Palace of Culture and Science. Why? Because that is the only place from which you cannot see the Palace of Culture and Science! Poles thoroughly dislike this building—the "wedding-cake

The not-so-beloved Palace of Culture and Science dominates the scene in Warsaw.

skyscraper"—as it was a gift from Jozef Stalin and thus symbolizes Soviet domination.

Rejoicing in their relatively newborn democracy, middle aged Poles (the forty-somethings) often disguise their present struggles for jobs, money, and the children's needs with stories of past horrors—how it took eight weeks to get an application form for a passport, a year for a television set; how one had to pay a bribe just to keep his or her place on the waiting list. Older Poles, however, remember the good old times of the 1970s, when foreign loans gave their country access to many material goods at cheap prices.

It is their fervent nationalism that has sustained the Poles through history. Foreign invasions and partitions could not kill their instinct to survive, even when they were nationless for a hundred years or when they were massacred by the Nazis. The Poles not only withstood the persecution but arose to lead their neighbors in bringing down Communism.

Polish optimism is renowned. For example, there are some who insist it never rains on Saturdays. The traditional saying goes: "Saturday is the day the Blessed Virgin does the celestial washing. Therefore it cannot rain."

The Poles are fond of their eccentricity. More than a few will tell the story of Karol Radziwill, an eighteenth-century Polish nobleman who was fond of drinking. Apparently, his favorite activity was shooting at bison that had been catapulted into the air. In his chapel, music was played by an orchestra dressed as Turkish soldiers. When people criticized him for living more grandly than the king, he said, "I live like a Radziwill. The king can live how he likes."

HOME OWNERSHIP

Poland has made significant economic progress since the fall of Communism. Apartments are easier to find now than during the days of Communist rule, when only members of the ruling party could live in more than one room. More Poles are now able to obtain a mortgage and as of 2007, 58 percent of people owned their own homes and 38 percent rented; 40 percent lived in detached houses, and 55 percent lived in apartments.

Poles are now taking advantage of modern financial institutions and services. Major US and European banks operate hundreds of branches in Poland, even in the small cities. Gone are the days of stuffing money into socks in the chimney or into mattresses. Being tied into the global commercial finance world has its plusses and minuses, however.

People with mortgages in Swiss francs protest the hike in their monthly payments. They are in front of the presidential palace in Warsaw, in January 2015.

In 2015, several hundred homeowners demonstrated in Warsaw against the high financial burden of their mortgages, demanding that the banks provide some kind of relief. Their particular mortgages had been issued in Swiss francs, which had been a popular and affordable type of loan in Poland, Hungary, and Romania during the real estate boom in the early 2000s. But a recent policy shift by the Swiss National Back caused the value of these franc-based mortgages to skyrocket. The currency explanation is complicated, but the outcome is that people's monthly mortgage payments became suddenly much higher, and Polish officials worried that vast numbers of homeowners would default on, or stop paying, their mortgages.

CHILDREN

There is a street in Warsaw called Kubus Puhatek, or Winnie the Pooh, named at the request of the local children. (Who wouldn't want to have such a charming address?)

Polish children learn etiquette from an early age. Some boys are still taught to kiss a woman's hand in greeting. But gone are the days when Polish children would shower visitors with questions about "life in the West." Most Polish children have access to the same books and magazines, television and radio programs, and computer games that children in other European

Students study in the library.

countries have. Polish children also dress the way their peers in the United States do and have similar ambitions. Many learn English as a second language, starting in kindergarten. Almost all are Internet savvy.

School hours were shortened when the country's economic transformation began. Many children finish the school day before their parents get home from work. There is unease about the number of kids who wander the streets with nothing worthwhile to do. Videos, DVDs, computer games, and the Internet are popular pursuits among young people.

In the Polish countryside, children dream of going to the city. Originally, they went in search of work, but now many are attracted by the modern entertainments unavailable in rural life.

The legal age in Poland is eighteen. Only then does a young person gain the full rights of Polish citizenship.

EDUCATION

Poles greatly value education and knowledge. As early as 1773, they established a national education commission, the first central non-religious education authority in Central Europe. It started a system of primary and secondary schools plus higher education that has lasted to today; the only addition has been pre-primary school.

Pre-primary school, for children ages three to six, is not free, but from age seven, education is compulsory and free. Poland has a 99.7-percent literacy rate, which is pretty hard to beat.

Polish culture and history are strongly emphasized in the school curriculum, as are foreign languages and computer skills. High-school students specialize and can choose from a range of subjects, including

German, English, biology, chemistry, and mathematics. Lessons last from 8 a.m. to 1 p.m. or 2:30 p.m. at the latest).

There are about 310 privately owned universities and colleges and 138 state schools of higher education and Poland's university enrollment rate is the fourth highest among Organization for Economic Cooperation and Development nations. Tuition is free for students accepted to university.

Poland is proud of its universities. The Jagiellonian University in Krakow was founded in 1364, making it the oldest in Central Europe after the University of Prague. Two of the Jagiellonian University's most famous students are the Renaissance astronomer Nicolaus Copernicus (1473-1543) and Karol Wojtyla, who became Pope John Paul II. The Flying University, founded in 1882, gave Polish women the chance to pursue higher education. Classes were held in people's homes and moved from one apartment to another, hence the name Flying University.

Jagiellonian University in Krakow is the oldest university in Poland. This building houses the physics and astronomy departments.

Government cost cutting has affected education in Poland. Teachers under Communist rule were accustomed to having a job for life, but now they have to produce results to keep their jobs. Reduced government spending has also meant fewer teaching hours and sometimes smaller paychecks. Schools may use a double shift, with some students studying in the morning and others in the afternoon, so that fewer teachers are needed. Tightened budgets mean that some optional classes have been discontinued. Schools have to find sponsors or engage in fund-raising activities to get extra income. The popularity of private schools has increased as they grow in number and quality. As study loans become available and people value learning more, even adults are attending classes to gain new knowledge and skills. Particularly popular are technology training programs.

STATE OF HEALTH CARE

Health-care workers in Warsaw demand higher pay and more government funds for the health care sector. They are carrying a stretcher with a banner reading "Agony."

The Polish Socialist state used to assure its citizens of full medical care at no cost. Like the bland assertion of full employment, that was only propaganda. The general health of the people was low, and medical standards were poor. Poles went to a pharmacy if they felt unwell and consulted the pharmacist there. They were reluctant to go to a hospital where there were too few beds, insufficient medicines, and sometimes unsanitary conditions.

Today Poland has compulsory, state-funded healthcare that provides medical care to all. The system is funded in two ways, through the government and through mandatory individual contributions, through employers, to the state healthcare insurance. Employees pay around 8.5 percent of gross salary to the National Health Fund (*Narodowy Fundusz Zdrowia*, or *NFZ*) and this is deducted directly from each person's salary.

In general, medical staff throughout Poland is extremely well trained. But there can be long waits to see doctors. Poland has a lower number of doctors and nurses than most Western European countries, with the majority of doctors located in cities and large towns.

Poles who can afford it supplement with private insurance. There are many doctors and specialists who have private practices which operate outside the state system. Private healthcare is used by more people in Poland than in other EU member states.

SUNDAYS ARE FOR FAMILY

In Poland, Sunday is a day of rest. For rural families, Sunday may start with a bath for everyone. Then father puts on a suit and polished pointed shoes, mother shows off a traditional dress with floral patterns, and the children are smart in clean jeans and a freshly ironed shirt with a bright scarf. The house is tidied, chores are done, and off they go to 11 a.m. Mass.

People selling flowers or local produce seize the chance to set up their stalls in the churchyard, where there will be a ready crowd after the Mass. The men will gather for a drink, and the children hang out.

But the women return home to prepare lunch. The long, leisurely Sunday afternoon includes a promenade down the main street, with youths racing their bikes through the park and couples strolling hand-in-hand and eating ice cream. Some lean out from their apartment balconies to share the sun with their friends.

A wedding couple has pictures taken in the market square in Krakow.

MARRIAGE

Poles have a deep respect for family. What could be more splendid than a wedding, that ceremony to mark the start of a new family? Celebration is obligatory. An invited guest might take three days off work to attend.

Shots of vodka and a loaf of bread topped with salt are traditional wedding fare.

Historically, a family that could not afford the cost of a wedding might sell a cow to pay for it.

In the old days, a landowner's permission might be needed for a peasant to marry—and he would be an honored guest at the festivities. Traditional rituals include the blessing of the bride and groom by the parents before the actual church ceremony; greenery on the bride's headdress representing her virginity; gates of greenery through which the couple pass on their way home from church; and the ceremonial greeting of the bride by her mother-in-law with bread and salt for her new home. Such customs are not always observed today, especially in the towns, where the bride wears a white gown and the groom a dark suit in Western style.

Poles traditionally believe that the success of a marriage will depend on the lavishness of the hospitality and the natural gaiety of the wedding feast. The band must not stop playing, so bridesmaids feed the musicians, while others pour sips of alcohol into their mouths!

In the evening, the couple are conducted to their bedroom to the sounds of a slow and solemn polonaise, danced to by the heads of the families and the married women. The following morning comes the "capping" of the new bride, the first wearing of the traditional headgear that shows she has joined the ranks of married people. By custom, the bride tries to put off that moment: she defends herself and throws off the cap; finally she agrees with much bitter sobbing, to show her reluctance to leave her family. This solemn ritual is no place for frivolous dancing or laughter.

The polonaise and "capping," like other traditional rituals, are seldom observed by modern couples in larger towns, but they are still practiced in the countryside.

THE LAST DAYS

Social security for the elderly is provided by a combination of public and private pension insurance, and like health care, is compulsory for basic benefits. For those who can afford it, a higher level of benefits can be purchased privately.

The family unit is important throughout life. There are few homes for the aged; the family looks after their aged relatives. Grandparents look after the grandchildren after school when the parents are working.

When there was a death in the family, relatives were required by tradition to wear black for a year. Nowadays a black mourning band suffices. A lot of money is spent on graves and tombstones. After the funeral, the wake is another good Polish party. There will be tribute speeches and toasts in spontaneous celebration of the departed's life.

Graves are adorned with flowers in a typical cemetery in Poland.

INTERNET LINKS

www.usatoday.com/story/news/world/2014/08/12/ozy-polish-education-system/13949837
"What the U.S. could learn from the Polish education system," is a 2014 article on *USA Today*.

www.theguardian.com/world/2011/apr/04/new-europe-poland-family-life
"New Europe: the life of a Polish family" is an interesting look at a typical young Polish family.

www.polandforvisitors.com/travel_poland/culture
A quick overview of the Polish lifestyle is offered on this tourism site.

RELIGION

The St. Paraskewa Greek Orthodox Church in Kwiaton, near the Slovakia border, is a World Heritage Site.

8

POLAND IS ONE OF THE MOST Catholic nations in the world. At least 87.5 percent of the population is Roman Catholic, which makes Poland more uniformly Catholic than Italy, Ireland, or Spain. Although it is not the state religion—the Polish Constitution guarantees freedom of religion—the Catholic faith is central to the life of the Polish people. They count their history as beginning when King Mieszko I was baptized and so adopted Christianity for Poland in 966 CE. The oldest churches in the country preserve medieval Christian architecture. Six wooden churches in Malopolskie dating back to the Middle Ages are on the UNESCO World Heritage list.

FIERCE CATHOLICS

Throughout history, Poland has been a fiercely defended outpost of Christian Europe. As Christianity spread through the Roman Empire,

According to a 2012 survey, 6 percent of Poles said they attended religious services more than once a week; 48 percent said they attended once a week; 18 percent went once or twice a month; 20 percent went a few times a year, and 8 percent did not go at all. These numbers represent a strong drop in church attendance over the previous ten years.

differences of opinion arose between east and west. In 1054 CE the Orthodox Church broke ties with Rome. Russia aligned itself with the Orthodox movement, but Poland stayed firmly aligned with Rome.

Persecution can strengthen faith, and in the case of Poland, four decades of Communist-supported atheism failed completely. Instead, those years saw a religious revival, linked joyously with the election of a Polish pope, Pope John Paul II (1920—2005) in 1978. The Solidarity trade union was seen as an expression of the Christian values of brotherhood and the dignity of work.

CHURCH AND LIFE

On Sundays, Polish Catholics flood their churches, which may hold three or four services, called Masses, to accommodate the congregations. On festival days, processions may block country roads for miles, carrying colorful banners with appeals to the Virgin Mary embroidered in gold and silver thread: "Holy Mary, Mother of God, protect us; do not abandon us, we are your children."

Lanes and road crossings in the countryside are lined with thousands of shrines, which are lovingly cared for and often adorned with ribbons and garlands. In winter, people trudge through the mud and snow, decorating shrines with twining boughs and paper flowers. If a shrine carries a cross, it commemorates a death. If it has a figure of the Madonna, it celebrates healing or a life saved. In most Polish homes there is an icon of the Virgin Mary or a portrait of Pope John Paul II, or both. The church is the heart of the village.

Mass is a joyous gathering for Roman Catholics in Poland. Sunday is a holy day of obligation—and so are major Christian feast days. Fulfilling their religious obligation with enthusiasm is nothing strange for Poles. People can be found at prayer in almost every church. In 1966 Poland celebrated its thousandth year as a Christian country.

Religion is not merely a comfort to older folk. Many young Poles are involved in the life of the church community. However, as is the case in most Western European nations, church attendance is falling among the under-thirty crowd in Poland.

Not that the Church isn't trying to connect with its younger members. In 2013, Pope Francis, who was made a cardinal by John Paul II, announced that World Youth Day, the Church's—and the world's—largest religious gathering of young people, would be held in Krakow in 2016.

Nevertheless, research indicates that the Church's power in Poland seems to be fading some. Some analysts suggest that now that the oppression of communism has lifted, Poles may no longer feel the need to cling to the Church for strength and resistance. Others suggest the influence of twenty-first century values is undermining the devotion to the church, particularly among the young.

TWO TWENTIETH-CENTURY HEROES

In 1952 Cardinal Stefan Wyszynski, the primate of the Roman Catholic Church in Poland, was exiled to a monastery as part of the Communist attack on the Church. In 1956 the Polish party leader, Wladyslaw Gomulka, freed Wyszynski because he needed his support. Wyszynski promptly demanded that the teaching of religion be reinstated in schools, that religious publications be restarted, and that imprisoned priests be released. All his demands were granted.

It was a strange partnership. The cardinal and the Communist were the only two leaders the Poles would trust. Wyszynski was not supporting the Communist regime; he was supporting national unity. Without Wyszynski, much of the Polish spirit would never have survived. His vital work continued through years of protest, right up to the formation of Solidarity.

In 1989, the Catholic Church began the process toward the beatification of Cardinal Wyszynski, who has been granted the title "Servant of God."

Cardinal Stefan Wyszynski in 1970

When Karol Jozef Wojtyla appeared on the steps of Saint Peter's Basilica in Rome as Pope John Paul II, his first words were "Non abbiate paura!" ("Be not afraid!") It was 1978. Poland was in the grip of food shortages and price increases, strikes and arrests. The first non-Italian pope in more than four hundred years and the first ever Polish pope, Wojtyla believed his election was some form of divine compensation for the sufferings of Poland.

Wojtyla was born on May 18, 1920, in Wadowice, about 20 miles (32 km) southwest of Krakow. His mother died when he was nine years old; his older brother died when he was twelve. His father became an admirable source of stability. Wojtyla recalls how seeing his father on his knees in prayer had a decisive influence on his early years. Sadly, his father died during the Nazi occupation. Before reaching age twenty-one, Wojtyla had already lost the people he loved most.

When Wojtyla was at the Jagiellonian University in Krakow, the teachers were deported to concentration camps. He chose to train as a priest, which could be done only in the strictest secrecy. In order to stay in the area where college teaching was done in secret, Wojtyla worked in a stone quarry that supplied the sulfur factory in Krakow. Wojtyla became a priest, as his mother had hoped, and his career prospered. He eventually became the archbishop of Krakow and later a cardinal.

On October 16, 1978, Cardinal Wojtyla was elected Holy Father of the Roman Catholic Church, becoming Pope John Paul II. He was the first Slav pope. During his papacy, he was widely beloved, but he did have his critics. He was a strong proponent of human rights, and, naturally, was strongly anti-communist. For these stands, he was almost universally applauded. He was opposed to the death penalty, unlike some popes before him, and some people found that stance troubling. Others didn't like his support for the church's opposition to the use of birth control and any consideration of the ordination of women. He was also criticized by some people for failing to adequately address some of the scandals rocking the Catholic Church at the time.

But these debates did not diminish the broad adoration for him in his homeland. John Paul II visited Poland in 1979, 1983, and 1987, emphasizing that the Church, not Communism, truly ruled Poland. Millions traveled to see him and hear him preach, and there was a great surge of joy throughout the country. After the fall of Communism, the pope made several pastoral visits to the country: in 1991, 1997, 1999, and 2002.

After John Paul died in 2005, the church waived the usual five-year waiting period and began the process of beatification. The Polish pope was declared a saint on April 27, 2014.

Beatification is an official declaration by the pope that a deceased person is in Heaven and is the proper subject of religious veneration. It is the first step on the road to sainthood.

Another Polish Church leader was Jerzy Popieluszko, who rose from humble beginnings as a farmer's son to become a fiery pro-Solidarity preacher. Father Popieluszko's outspoken comments during the days of martial law embarrassed the Communist state.

Despite being threatened and arrested by security forces, Father Popieluszko continued to speak out against the regime. On October 19, 1984, security forces kidnapped and murdered him. His driver escaped, so details of what had happened became known. The people were enraged and started riots. The government tried the murderers and sent the two ring-leaders to prison for twenty-five years.

Popieluszko's funeral became a Solidarity demonstration. His grave and the church he served, Saint Stanislaw Kostka, in northern Warsaw remain Solidarity shrines.

On June 6, 2010, Popieluszko was recognized as a martyr by the Catholic Church and was beatified. More than 100,000 people attended the open-air Mass in his honor in Warsaw.

The holiest shrine in Poland is the Jasna Gora, or "Shining Mountain," the Pauline monastery at Czestochowa. The chapel of Jasna Gora houses the miraculous image of the Black Madonna, Poland's most treasured icon.

Legend has it that the image of the Black Madonna was painted by Saint Luke on a tabletop made from dark cypress wood by Saint Joseph himself. The "black" quality of the image is merely the result of the aging of the pigments used. Rescued from the ruins of Jerusalem in 70 CE, the icon was taken to Byzantium and presented to King Constantine. In the fourteenth century, it was presented to the Polish king Casimir, who put it in Czestochowa for safe keeping. Brigands once tried to steal the picture, but when they reached the German border, their horses, "moved by a miraculous force," refused to go any farther. So the picture was returned to the monastery.

Poles believe the real miracle took place about 350 years ago when a Swedish invasion swept over Poland but failed to capture the monastery. The monks, with a handful of Polish troops, held out until the Swedish commander called off the siege. It seems his soldiers refused to go on fighting. They swore that "their own bullets came back at them, bouncing off the monastery walls." They said they saw a woman in a blue cloak floating above the shrine and covering the fortress with her mantle. They were convinced that heavenly forces were on the side of the monks. Perhaps even more miraculously, the shrine of the Black Madonna emerged safely from both Nazi and Communist occupations.

Every August, hundreds of thousands of pilgrims make the journey to Czestochowa—many entirely on foot, no matter where they start—and visit the high-domed Gothic chapel to kneel before the black-and-silver altar of the Virgin Mary. The chapel walls are hung with countless offerings in gratitude for healing miracles—silver plaques with a name and date, shaped like a heart, an eye, a limb, or even discarded crutches.

UNUSUAL CHURCHES AND MONASTERIES

Poland has more churches and priests today than before the war. In such a religious-minded nation, it is not surprising that there are some very impressive places of worship.

Most unusual must be the underground Chapel of the Blessed Kings hewn in crystal rock at the ancient salt mine of Wieliczka. Everything in the large ornate chapel is carved from salt: stairs, banisters, altar, and chandeliers. The acoustics are so good that the chapel is also used occasionally for concerts.

In Krakow is the Church of Saint Andrew, topped with twin baroque spires. The silver pulpit inside is a masterpiece in the shape of a ship manned by angelic mariners, as is the case in many Polish churches. Nuns attend services hidden behind a grille in the gallery.

On Silver Mountain (so called because of the silver bark of the birches) west of Krakow stands the church and hermitage of the Camaldolese monks at Bielany. Here lives a strict monastic order from Italy whose motto is

A section of a wall sculpture in the main hall of an underground chapel in the Wieliczka Salt Mine. The mine has been a UNESCO World Heritage Site since 1979.

The church and hermitages of the Camaldolese Monastery are a serene place of contemplative life.

Memento mori ("Remember you must die"). Monks live in seclusion, dressed in cream-colored robes, each with his own tiny cottage and vegetable garden that is his only source of food. They meet for common meals only five times a year. Except for times of prayer, they maintain a vow of silence. The white limestone church and the crypt (where bodies are sealed inside stone niches) may be visited by men, but women are only admitted only twelve days a year during major religious celebrations, which is a recent change from the previous once a year.

RELIGIOUS TOLERANCE

Open-minded in most matters, Poles have a fairly narrow view when it comes to religion. A Protestant can be regarded as a foreigner. Yet Poland used to be famous for its religious tolerance. Those with unorthodox beliefs, whether Christian or not, found hospitality here.

It was to Poland that the oppressed Jews of Western Europe came for a haven, followed by the persecuted Bohemian Brotherhood (a Christian group formed in Bohemia in 1467). For several centuries, Poland had Europe's greatest concentration of Jews, secure in their own religious, cultural, and intellectual life. Today, there are places of worship for Protestants, Catholics, Jews, Muslims, and Buddhists. There are also churches of the Eastern Orthodox creed with their double-barred, slanting crucifix.

Yet suspicion of those of a different faith is deep-rooted in Poland's history. In 1668 the Sejm declared that anybody who converted from Catholicism to another branch of Christianity would be exiled. Non-Catholics could not become Polish nobles—and thus members of the Sejm. Of course, not everybody obeyed such rules.

Poles today are free to worship as they please. Poland has perhaps a million non-Catholic believers, including an established Lutheran church. There are a small number of Methodists and Baptists, and a few thousand Muslim Tartars, but the Roman Catholic Church remains monolithic.

INTERNET LINKS

www.pbs.org/wgbh/pages/frontline/shows/pope
PBS Frontline presents an in-depth multimedia presentation, "John Paul II: The Millennial Pope."

visnews-en.blogspot.com/2014/02/pope-francis-to-polish-bishops-church.html
Vatican Information Service presents Pope Francis' message to Polish Bishops in 2014.

www.spiegel.de/international/europe/influence-of-catholic-church-on-the-decline-in-poland-a-843694.html
An article in Spiegel Online examines "Crisis of Faith: The Catholic Church's Fading Influence in Poland."

www.pri.org/stories/2013-09-27/story-fight-catholicism-poland
"Story: The fight for Catholicism is on in Poland" is offered in print and audio on PRI.

The front pages of newspapers reveal the Polish language at work in everyday life.

9

SOME FORTY MILLION PEOPLE SPEAK Polski. That's the Polish word for Polish, meaning the language. Polish uses the same alphabet as West European languages, with the exception of one letter and some extra accented letters.

Polish is a Western Slavic language, along with Czech and Slovak. Russian is also a Slavic language, though it belongs to the East Slavic group and uses the very different Cyrillic alphabet. This double group of languages, often known as Balto-Slavic, is spoken by about 300 million people, more

Powodzenia! (poh-voh-DJEN-ya) means "Good Luck!" As a good luck gesture, Poles hold the fist with the thumb concealed inside, and have the saying "I'm holding thumbs for you."

In Polish, the letter *J* makes a *Y* sound, as on these police vests.

than half of whom speak Russian. As the Polish language differs slightly in different areas, the standard form of Polish is based on the dialect spoken in the Wielkopolskie region of western Poland.

Not everyone in Poland speaks Polish at home. The Ukrainian and Belarusian minorities are bilingual. They speak Polish well, yet their home languages mark them as a separate language group.

Large white letters say KAZDY SIE LICZY ("Everyone counts") on a street in Lodz.

LANGUAGE UNITES A NATION

The earliest recorded use of Polish appears in twelfth-century Church documents. There are many hymns, sermons, psalters, and law-court records dating from the early Middle Ages (fourteenth and fifteenth centuries). Despite the fall of the Polish state in the late eighteenth century, Polish culture continued to develop. Language united the nation, yet local dialects reflecting former tribal patterns remain significant. For example, there are clearly recognized dialects known as Silesian, Great Polish, Little Polish, and Mazovian. Poles from Warsaw will find it hard to understand Poles from a village in the Tatra Mountains.

LANGUAGES IN SCHOOL

At times in Polish history, it was forbidden to use Polish in schools and offices. Adam Mickiewicz, one of Poland's most admired poets, grew up in the 1820s, when the imperial Russian government was determined to eliminate the Polish language and culture. To succeed, a Pole was expected to learn Russian and convert to Russian Orthodoxy. Similarly, under Communist domination, Russian was mandated in all schools from grade five to grade twelve, and a course in Russian was compulsory in any university degree course.

For the Poles, their language has become more than just a means of communication; it is a symbol of the continued existence of the Polish nation.

Here are some basic Polish expressions:

tak (tahk) . . . . *yes*

nie (nye) . . . . *no*

prosze (PRO-she) . . . . *please*

dzienkuje (jen-KOO-yeah) . . . . . . *thank you*

przepraszam (pshe-PRASH-am) . . . . *sorry, or excuse me*

do widzenia (do vid-ZEN-ia) . . . . . *goodbye*

When the Communist state tried to add new words and expressions to the Polish language, the Poles developed their own underground version of the language in which they could voice their hatred of Russian domination.

Poles today want to also learn English, since it is a global language, and German, to build economic ties with their western neighbor. In fact, English is becoming seen as a sign of sophistication. Knowing English is a status symbol and helps career prospects. English teaching has become one of the most thriving businesses in Poland.

EXPRESSIONS IN COMMON USE

If you hear a Pole saying "Jen Dobry," it is not someone's name, but a greeting, "Dzien dobry!" (jen DO-bri), which means "Good morning!" Before a drive, a Pole may wish you "Szerokiej drogi!" (she-ROK-yay DRO-gi), or "Have a wide road!"

Unlike modern English, Polish has two forms of address, polite, or formal; and casual, intimate, or informal. A familiar form of address among friends and relations is *ty* or "you" (like the French *tu* or the German *du*). However, *ty* (ti) is not used when greeting older people or those in important positions, for whom the correct forms of address are *pan* (pan), or "sir," and *pani* (pa-NEE), or "madam." When addressing someone you know, it is impolite to use his or her surname. There is automatic respect for those with professional

A road sign shows which highways to take to the cities of Bydgoszcz, Pila, Warsaw, Wroclaw, and Katowice.

qualifications. For example, a doctor is called *panie doktorze* (pa-NYE dok-TO-zhe), or "sir doctor."

Some words you will recognize easily, such as auto, hotel, and stop. Many familiar greetings come from the strong religious element in Polish life. Villagers greet each other with "May Jesus Christ be praised," to which the response will be "Forever and ever." *Szczesc Boze* (shCHEshch BOH-zhe), meaning "God bless you," is a common Polish goodbye.

PRONUNCIATION

Knowing a few words in Polish goes a long way in making friends in Poland, so it is worth the trouble making sense of what may look like a jumble of consonants without vowels. The complexity of the Polish language goes back to the time when Poland disappeared from the map. Teachers were determined to save every detail of the old language. As a result, Polish did not really go through the same process that modernized and simplified so many European languages.

Polish vowels are pronounced as follows (the last three are unique to the Polish language):

    a . . . .as in "papa"
    e . . . .as in "ten"
    i . . . .as in "teeth"
    ó . . . .as in "coat"
    u . . . .as in "cuckoo"
    y . . . .as in "sit"
    a . . . .nasalized, as in the French on
    e . . . .nasalized, as in the French un
    ó . . . .the same as Polish u

There is also the diphthong ie (y-e), so that nie wiem, meaning "I don't know," sounds like "NY-eh VY-em."

Consonants sound mostly the way they do in English, except for the following:

    c . . . .pronounced "ts" or "tz"
    j . . . .soft, like the "y" in "yes"
    w . . . .sounds like "v"

There are thirty-two letters and forty-five sounds in the Polish language. The written form may look complicated, but the sounds each letter represents are at least consistent. The stress, or beat, almost always falls on the next to last syllable. Three genders—masculine, feminine, and neuter—create different cases and structures for some verbs, nouns, and adjectives. Nouns may change with a preceding preposition, so while the Polish word *miasto* (mya-STO) means "town," it becomes *do miasta* (do mya-STA) if you want to say "to the town."

As in German, which is a related language, some Polish consonants are softened when they come at the end of a word, so *b, d, g, w,* and *z* become *p, t, k, f,* and *s* respectively. The combination *ch* sounds guttural, as in the

Polish has many sibilant sounds. In any language, sibilants are sounds that hiss, sizzle, and chatter. (In fact, those three English words contain sibilants.) In English, the common sibilants are the sounds of s, z, sh, ch, soft g, and j, as in the words so, zoo, she, cheap, gee, and jeep. English also has a sibilant that occurs only in the interior of a word: si as in vision. Words containing sibilant sounds are sharp and intense; they have a certain harsh quality that attracts attention. (Notice how all the adjectives describing sibilants in that sentence contain sibilants.)

Polish has more of these sounds, which can make the language itself sound scratchy to the unfamiliar ear, and which challenge the untrained tongue trying to speak it. In Polish, the sounds ch, cz, rz, sz, szcz are pronounced something like this: ch is a rough h sound, gargled in the throat; cz is like a chipped t sound; rz is like a z sound; sz is close to a sss sound; and szcz, as mentioned above, is something like shht or shhtch. These are approximate descriptions, as the sounds have no English equivalent.

Scots word *loch*, and the accented ń goes wobbly, as in *canyon* or the Spanish *mañana*. The daunting combination *szcz* is easy to cope with if you remember the words "Polish chair," and use the "sh-ch" sound in the middle.

There is also a specially marked letter with a stroke across it: ł. This sounds like "w" and has the effect of making Władysław sound like "VWAH-DI-SWAV" and Łódz sound like "WOOCH" (ó with that accent sounds like "oo"). To pronounce the name of the founding leader of Solidarity, Lech Wałęsa, say "LEK vaWENsa."

A VERY HANDY LANGUAGE

Poles shake hands at every meeting, even with lifelong friends. A warm friendship gets an embrace as well. The older or more senior person will give the first greeting and expects a similarly courteous reply. A woman may hold out her hand for a man to kiss in greeting. "I kiss your hand," he says, in old-style courtesy. In the street, a man always walks on the left of the woman.

Europeans tend to use their hands freely as they talk (although the

English tend to put their hands in their pockets). Poles gesticulate in much the same way as the French and Italians. Just occasionally, such sign language can be misunderstood. When Polish soldiers and airmen reached England during World War II, for example, they happily gave the V-sign for victory. Unfortunately, the Polish sign is the opposite of the British one (the back of the hand is shown), and some people thought they were being rude!

There is a mildly rude gesture of defiance made by brandishing a fist while grabbing the inside of the elbow with the other hand. It is known as the Kozakiewicz gesture, in affectionate memory of the Polish pole-vaulter who was booed by the Russians at the 1980 Olympics in Moscow. Having made the jump that earned him the gold medal, he turned to the Russian crowd in full view of the television cameras and made this sign.

Politician Jaroslaw Kaczinski flashes the "V for Victory" sign in 2012.

INTERNET LINKS

www.omniglot.com/writing/polish.htm
Omniglot is a good starting point for introducing the Polish language.

www.staypoland.com/polish.htm
Stay Poland, a tourism site, offers an overview of Polish for beginners.

onestoppolish.com/useful_polish_phrases.htm
This site offers a list of common phrases with audio for each one.

ARTS

Polish folk art designs, such as in this cut-paper art called Wycinanki, are wonderfully colorful and whimsical.

10

WHEN POLAND WAS DIVIDED among its neighbors at the end of the eighteenth century, the arts played the role of preserving the nation and its identity. Similarly, during the repressive four and a half decades of Communist control in the twentieth century, protest against the state was voiced chiefly through theater and painting. Traditional costumes, dance, and decorative arts were kept alive in local regions, but the dull demands of industrialization led to their decline. Today, tourism has encouraged fresh artistic creativity.

Vibrant folk arts and regional specialities exhibit marvelous expressions of Polish tradition and spirit: the glass paintings by the Zakopane mountain folk; the black pottery of Kielce; the red, sequined folk costumes from Krakow; multicolored cloth from Lowicz; the lacework of Koniakow; intricate paper cutouts, called Wycinanki (at left) from Kurpie; and the brass bands of Silesia. The village of Zalipie is famous for the floral paintings that decorate its houses. It even has an annual competition of the best painted houses.

In 2010, every baby born in Warsaw received a commemorative Chopin onesie shirt in celebration of the two hundredth anniversary of the birth of Polish composer Frederic Chopin. More than sixteen thousand were handed out.

A LAND OF MUSIC

Music is alive and thriving in Poland. Such names as Frederic Chopin, Ignace Jan Paderewski, and Artur Rubinstein are nearly synonymous with Poland. International competitions, such as the Frederic Chopin piano competition and the Henryk Wieniawski violin competition, give added status. Poland also has many conservatories, music schools, and music centers, as well as music societies and magazines. Warsaw stages opera and ballet performances, chamber concerts, and recitals every night, and regular performances by the national philharmonic orchestra. The city also plays host to the Jazz Jamboree, the oldest, most celebrated jazz festival in Eastern Europe.

But all that started with village musicians. Music based on the fiddle, pan pipes, or single-reed bagpipe (or in the Kurpie forest region, an accordion with a foot pump) created the dance rhythms of the mazurka and polka, which are still played in the traditional style in many villages, often for weddings and festivals. There is a folk festival each year at Kazimierz on the banks of the Vistula River that is very popular, attracting many young Poles to participate.

A street musician plays his accordion in the old market of Posen.

FAMOUS MUSICIANS

ARTUR RUBINSTEIN (1887—1982) was a delightful, slightly old-fashioned showman—for many years, he was the world's best-loved concert pianist, well-known as an interpreter of the Romantic composers. He often performed Brahms, Schumann, and Chopin, and his recordings, made directly without correction—unlike in modern recordings—remain dazzling. Born in Lodz, he made his professional debut at age ten with the Berlin Philharmonic Orchestra. During World War II, Rubenstein, a Jew, moved to the United States, and became a US citizen in 1946.

WITOLD LUTOSLAWSKI (1913—1994), a Polish composer of the older generation compared to more contemporary composers as Penderecki, Krauze, and Gorecki, remains highly popular with concert-goers. His "Variations on a Theme of Paganini" was composed in 1941, during the Nazi occupation of Warsaw, when he was a café pianist and played duets with a friend after working hours. But he is best known for his stunning *Cello Concerto*, crammed with discordant orchestral exuberance.

FREDERIC CHOPIN (1810—1849) made his debut as a pianist at age eight. The son of a French father and a Polish mother, he lived in Warsaw until the age of twenty, and then made his home in Paris. There, he built a reputation for himself in fashionable salons as both composer and pianist.

The Frederic Chopin monument, which now stands in Warsaw's Royal Baths Park, was designed by Polish sculptor and painter Waclaw Szymanowski in 1907.

Although he never lived in Poland again, Chopin continued to draw inspiration from his homeland, incorporating Slavic folk tunes and rhythms in his work. He revolutionized piano playing, concentrating on bravura solo pieces that show off the qualities of the instrument. His compositions for piano were characterized by an unusual lyrical and poetic quality. He died on October 17, 1849, and was buried in Paris. However, Warsaw still claims him as a native son, and grandly celebrated the two hundredth anniversary of his birth in 2010.

HENRYK MIKOLAJ GORECKI (go-RET-zki) (1933—2010) was a composer of contemporary classical music that is sometimes categorized as "holy minimalism." His Symphony No. 3 (1977) remains hugely popular. Also known as the *Symphony of Sorrowful Songs*, the piece features soprano solos in Polish in each of the three movements. The songs are about the separations of mothers and children during war: a fifteenth-century Polish lament by the Virgin Mary, a message written on the wall of a Gestapo cell during WWII, and a Silesian folk song about a mother searching for her son who had been killed by the Germans in the Silesian uprisings after WWI.

In 1992, a recording of Gorecki's symphony was recorded with American soprano Dawn Upshaw to commemorate the memory of those who perished during the Holocaust. The recording became a worldwide success, selling more than a million copies and greatly exceeding the typical lifetime sales of a recording of symphonic music by a twentieth-century composer.

LITERATURE

The earliest traces of Polish folklore and legend are preserved from medieval times. There exists, for example, the hymn chanted by King Jagiello's army before their victory over the Teutonic Knights at the Battle of Grunwald in 1410. Texts of Polish folk plays survive from the Renaissance.

The first public reference library on the European mainland was Bishop Zaluski's collection, which he donated to the Polish nation in 1747. The Sejm soon ordered printers to donate to the library the first copy of any book, and by the time the library was looted by the Russians in 1795, it contained more than 500,000 volumes.

A statue of poet Adam Mickiewicz on the main square in Krakow.

Writers are well-respected people in Poland. The nineteenth-century poet Adam Mickiewicz has the status of a national hero, and streets and squares are named after him. He wrote about Poland in a dark time and kept the flame of her spirit alive. His *Pan Tadeusz* ("Sir Thaddeus") and other works exerted a strong influence on future generations.

Polish-born prose writers have won the Nobel Prize in literature: Henryk Sienkiewicz for *Quo Vadis*, a story set in the time of Roman Emperor Nero; Wladyslaw Reymont, whose epic novel of Poland, *Chlopi*, is strong with local color and historical detail; and Czeslaw Milosz (1911—2004) for his poetry

FINDING LARGE TRUTHS IN SMALL THINGS

In 1996, Polish poet Wislawa Szymborska (VI-swava SHIM-bar-ska) (1923–2012) won the Nobel Prize in Literature. In her acceptance speech, she explained why movies are made about painters and musicians, but never about poets: "... poets are the worst. Their work is hopelessly unphotogenic. Someone sits at a table or lies on a sofa while staring motionless at a wall or ceiling. Once in a while this person writes down seven lines only to cross out one of them fifteen minutes later, and then another hour passes, during which nothing happens ... Who could stand to watch this kind of thing?"

Szymborska lived most of her life in Krakow. She studied Polish literature and sociology at Jagellonian University from 1945 until 1948. Although many of her poems are about war and terrorism—she did, after all, live through some of Poland's most difficult and terrifying years—they do so in ways that speak from the point of view of everyday life. Szymborska's work exposes her as a deeply personal poet who finds large truths in small, ordinary things.

> *After every war*
> *someone has to clean up.*
> *Things won't*
> *straighten themselves up, after all.*
> *—from "The End and the Beginning" (2001)*

For a poet of international reknown, she produced a relatively small body of work, fewer than 350 poems. When asked why she had published so few poems, she said, memorably, "I have a trash can in my home."

In 2011, shortly before she died, she was awarded Poland's highest civilian honor, the Order of the White Eagle, by President Bronisław Komorowski.

This Polish-born artist and author of children's books, born in 1936, remembers only too well how his family left his native Warsaw with Nazi bombs and shells falling all around. He was a young child at the time.

Now a citizen of Great Britain, Pienkowski is well known for his pop-up books, including Haunted House, Robot, Dinner Time, Good Night, *and seventeen others. A devout Catholic, Pienkowski has also illustrated two lovely picture books using delicate black silhouette figures against color-washed skies—one is about Christmas, the other about Easter. Anxious to make the story accessible to modern children, he shows Mary hanging up the washing as the Archangel Gabriel appears. "Maybe," he says, "this picture was based on an old Polish country saying that the sun shines when the Virgin hangs up her washing."*

and prose. His nonfiction book, *The Captive Mind* (1953), became a classic of anti-Stalinism. Wislawa Szymborska, who won in 1996, is known for the wit, irony, and deceptive simplicity of her poetry. Joseph Conrad, the popular author of English seafaring novels such as *Lord Jim*, was actually Jozef Korzeniowski, born of Polish parents in Ukraine.

Although the Communist government imposed severe restrictions on writers, it encouraged books and literacy. Today, the public libraries remain popular, and bookstalls spill onto sidewalks.

CINEMA

Despite tight state control and extreme censorship during Communism, Polish cinema produced some of the greatest films and filmmakers of the late twentieth century. Poland's first film company, Sphinx, was launched in 1909 and thrived in the inter-war period. After World War II, Polish film had a series of international hits by such directors as Andrzej Munk and Andrzej Wajda, who in 2000 received a lifetime achievement award from the Academy of Motion Picture Arts and Sciences.

Filmmaker Pawel Pawlikowski accepts the Academy Award for Best Foreign Film in Hollywood in 2015.

These and a few other filmmakers founded what became known as the Polish school of filmmaking. Oscar winner Roman Polanski, super successful in both Europe and Hollywood, continues to make films such as *The Pianist*—the moving biography of Wladyslaw Szpilman—and an adaptation of Charles Dickens's *Oliver Twist*. Jerzy Skolimowski, also well-regarded in Europe and the United States, cowrote Polanski's first feature film, *Knife in the Water*. Skolimowski has also won important prizes for his own movies, including *Walkover*, *Barrier*, and *Start*.

After the fall of communism, Poland's film industry went into a decline from lack of financial support. The number of movie theaters also fell, from 3,500 to about 800. In 2005, the country established a film institute and began granting funding to small movie productions, and the result has been positive. The number of movies being made in Poland jumped from seven in 2004 to fifty in 2015.

In 2015, the Polish film *Ida* won the Academy Award for Best Foreign Film. Directed by Pawel Pawlikowski, the movie was the first Polish film ever to achieve that recognition. The black and white film, set in 1962, is about a teenage girl who is preparing to become a nun when she learns that she is Jewish and her family was killed during the Holocaust.

THEATER

The Julius Slowacki Theater in Krakow is lit up on a winter night.

Live theater has always been popular in Poland. English traveling players used to visit there in medieval times. German translations of Shakespeare's plays were performed in Gdansk even during Shakespeare's lifetime. After the downfall of the Polish state, theater played an enormous role in preserving the Polish language and spirit. Drama was often used as a medium of political protest.

During the 1960s, the Polish Laboratory Theater in Wroclaw gained an international reputation for its experimental work. Under director Jerzy Grotowski, it toured Western Europe and the United States, and was acclaimed as an important new direction in theater. In January 1968, the Communist authorities banned as anti-Russian a production of *Forefather's Eve*, a play by the poet Adam Mickiewicz. Poles revered his work and protested violently.

Social comment is made on both sides of the footlights, for audiences are encouraged to respond vigorously. Irony and satire are strong elements in Polish theater. Working now in the United States, Polish playwright Janusz Glowacki uses shrewd observations on life in Communist Eastern Europe to entertain and enlighten theater audiences in the United States. In *Antigone in New York* (1993), a Polish thief and a Russian drunk are homeless New Yorkers determined to show their defiance of "the authorities."

There are three drama schools in Poland, and admission is very competitive. Poles flock to live entertainment at the country's many theaters, including puppet theaters, opera and musical theaters, and concert halls. Warsaw's Grand Theater houses the impressive Theater Museum.

A JUMBLE OF ARCHITECTURAL STYLES

One of the many decorated houses in an open-air museum in Zalopie

In a country that has so often been fought over, invaded, destroyed, and rebuilt, one would expect a variety of architectural styles. There are stern Romanesque churches, spired and fluted late-Gothic cathedrals, warm brick town halls, and ornate masterpieces of the Italian Renaissance and Baroque periods. Poles of the sixteenth and seventeenth centuries admired the beauty of Islamic art, which complemented the popular Baroque architecture. Eastern textiles replaced Flemish tapestries on the walls of manor houses. Onion-shaped turrets topped circular towers in the style of minarets.

The Poles themselves live comfortably amid the confusion of gaunt "Socialist realism" and decorative historical relics. They are more aware than the average tourist of just how many buildings that look historical are really clever reconstructions, especially in Warsaw. The Baroque Church of the Holy Cross in the capital city was completely rebuilt from paintings and old photographs after the city was destroyed in 1945. It is topped by a gigantic

Castles and palaces such as Wilanow Palace are undoubtedly jewels in the Polish architectural crown. Wawel Castle in Krakow is the most impressive. Built on a rocky embankment overlooking the Vistula River, its red-brick foundations, cream walls, and dark slate roofs mix Romanesque, Gothic, and Renaissance styles, and its ornate reception rooms recall ages of elegance long past.

Wawel is the first stop along the popular Eagle Nest Trail, a chain of medieval castles built by King Casimir the Great in the fourteenth century, which ends at the Royal Castle of Warsaw.

statue of Jesus Christ that was brought triumphantly back from Germany where it had been destined for scrap.

Many old houses such as those in the Old Town Square in Warsaw or most of Krakow have painted facades that often imitate carved classical styles. The same *trompe l'oeil* (fool the eye) painting was used inside many of the sumptuous palaces as well as those now being restored in Wilanow Palace in Warsaw. Yet perhaps even more breathtaking is the gilt-and-marble Baroque decoration in the bigger churches.

Although the city cathedrals and castles are undoubtedly impressive, it is the village houses that show the genuine Poland most clearly—red brick and tile, steep sloping roofs against the winter snow, and always the spire of the village church.

In Pomerania, in northern Poland, houses are wide but low, as if ducking down to avoid the wind. In Masuria, the lake region, they are smaller and sometimes thatched. In the mountains, houses are made of wood and have a pointed roof. The unsightly new square cottages with flat roofs that are seen almost everywhere are made of mass-produced building blocks. A recent development is the open-air museum, or *skansen* (SCAN-sen), which gathers models of traditional rural architecture to preserve the actual buildings. Wooden churches, mills, houses, and barns are equipped and decorated according to the style of the period. The country's oldest skansen, in Wdzydze Kiszewskie, Pomorskie, was founded in 1906.

INTERNET LINKS

www.nytimes.com/2015/02/24/movies/as-ida-wins-an-oscar-poland-ends-a-losing-streak.html?ref=topics&_r=0
The *New York Times* article about the movie *Ida* winning an Academy Award discusses the Polish film industry.

www.theguardian.com/music/2012/jun/07/polish-music-piotr-metz
"Polish music now: from punk-folk to hip-hop" discusses some of the contemporary pop music not discussed in the chapter, and includes many links.

www.nytimes.com/2010/11/13/arts/music/13gorecki.html?_r=0
An obituary for Henryk Gorecki, written in 2010, reviews his life and contributions.

www.newyorker.com/culture/culture-desk/wislawa-szymborska-the-happiness-of-wisdom-felt
"Wislawa Szymborska: The Happiness of Wisdom Felt" is an article from *The New Yorker*.

www.newrepublic.com/article/the-read/100479/wislawa-szymborska-nobel-poet-career
The New Republic offers "A Requiem to an Age of Brilliant Polish Poetry."

LEISURE

A child enjoys kayaking on the Rospuda River in northeastern Poland.

11

FOR SOME POLES, THE IDEA OF recreation means climbing K2, the most challenging peak in the Himalayan Mountains. (Indeed, Polish climbers have set records on that and others of Earth's highest peaks.) For other, only slightly less adventurous types, dressing up as a medieval knight and reenacting the 1410 Battle of Grunwald sounds like fun. Still others might prefer to bathe in a mixture of wine, milk, mud, and herbs at one of the country's many health and beauty spas or four-star hotels.

A wealth of possibilities exists, but naturally most Poles enjoy their leisure time in much the same way most people do. They visit friends, go shopping, read books, watch TV, surf the Internet, putter in the garden, listen to music, watch sports, or get some exercise.

SPORTS

Many Poles jog for sport and take part in local fun runs and serious marathons. There is a sports stadium in most towns; hockey, volleyball, basketball, and soccer are all popular.

Poles enjoy playing board games. Recent years have seen a boom in the market for board games, many of them based on Poland's history. The hit of the 2011-2012 season was reportedly a game called The Queue ("Waiting in Line"), set in the days of Communist Poland when Poles had to stand in line for almost any product.

The Polish National Football (soccer) Team is joined by small fans for the pregame hymn in the Dialog Arena in Lubin.

SOCCER The sport that Americans call soccer, the rest of the world calls football and the Polish call *pilka nozna*—that is the game children play in the streets and parents cheer on weekends. Soccer is the most popular sport in Poland, as it is in many other countries.

Some boys attend soccer practice for perhaps an hour after school, three times a week. Others play basketball or volleyball in the park. Yet others play "streetball," which is like basketball but with few players on each side (three, for example) and only one basket.

On Saturday mornings, people may close off part of a street and set up goalposts for soccer matches. Prizes may be donated by a sportswear manufacturer. Rain or shine, the matches are played through to a much-cheered finale. Soccer is the top spectator sport in Poland.

Poland has hundreds of amateur and professional teams, and leagues, at every level. The Polish National Football Team plays in international tournaments; it has qualified to play in the World Cup seven times. In 2012,

Poland cohosted the European Championship with Ukraine. It was a first-time honor for Poland to host a soccer event of that magnitude.

THE GREAT OUTDOORS

The Poles have a traditional love of the outdoor life. They have loved horses for centuries. With a history full of wild cavalry charges, it is no surprise how many riding stables and stud farms there are in Poland. Poland has a long tradition of breeding Arabian horses, particularly in the village of Janow Podlaski, close to the border with Belarus. Horse-riding, though obviously not an inexpensive pastime, remains popular. Hunting and fishing are carefully controlled with permit requirements.

A competitor jumps her horse in an international competition in Jaroszowska, Poland.

Older Poles especially love rifle shooting. Almost every large town has its marksmen's society. But nowhere is there as colorful a tradition as the Brotherhood of the Rooster in Krakow. The brotherhood parades through the city in traditional finery before going to the military firing range for the shoot-off with target rifles. This ritual dates back to when all citizens were expected to practice fighting skills, whether with bow, sword, or musket. A shooting competition evolved, with a wooden bird set on a high pole as the target. The one to shoot off the last remaining splinter became Rooster King for a year and paid no municipal taxes!

POLAND'S OLYMPIC RECORD

Poland was slow in building up to an Olympic sporting standard until the years after World War II. The leap to twenty-one medals in 1960 shows the emphasis placed on sports and training by the Communist regime.

After sixty-two nations, including the United States, boycotted the 1980 Olympics in Moscow because of the Soviet invasion of Afghanistan, the Soviet Union in turn boycotted the 1984 Olympics in Los Angeles. Most Communist

A HOME-GROWN CHAMP

At the 2010 Olympics in Vancouver, Canada, Polish cross-country skier Justyna Kowalczyk (b. 1983) beat out Norwegian Marit Bjorgen to take the gold in the 30 km classical sprint. With that victory, Kowalczyk became the first Polish Olympic cross-country ski champion. At the 2014 Winter Games in Sochi, Russia, she didn't disappoint and brought home another gold, this time in the 10 km classical—which she raced with a fractured foot! (She had broken her foot a mere two weeks before the race.) She was already a favorite in her country, having been named the Polish Sports Personality of the Year in 2009, 2010, 2011, and 2012.

After Sochi, Kowalczyk had earned a total of five Olympic medals: two golds, a silver, and two bronze. She is also the only skier to win the Tour de Ski four times in a row. That race is a cross-country skiing event held annually in Central Europe, modeled on the famous Tour de France for cycling. She is also one of two female skiers to win the FIS Cross-Country World Cup three times in a row.

Kowalczyk was born in Limanowa, Poland, a town in the south of the country, and began skiing at age ten. When she was fifteen, she began training and transferred to the sports high school in Zakopane, the famous ski resort city in the Tatra Mountains. By the age of twenty, the young skier was competing internationally. As if all her accomplishments weren't enough, in 2014, Kowalczyk earned a Ph.D. from Krakow's University of Physical Education.

countries, including Poland, had to follow suit. However, Poland has participated in all other Olympic Games, Winter and Summer.

Polish athletes have won a total of 291 Olympic medals, as of Sochi 2014, with track and field being the most successful sport. The Summer Games have brought Poland the most success by far, with 271 medals, including 64 golds. In the Winter Olympics, held since 1924, Poland has less to show for itself. It has taken home 20 medals, including 6 golds—and most of these have been won since 2002.

The ski jump in Zakopane opened in 1925.

WINTER SPORTS

Skiing is Poland's most popular winter sport. When winter comes, Poles make an overnight train journey to the High Tatras, waking up to the sight of snowcapped mountains and spruce forests. The Tatra range has lakes, waterfalls, hidden valleys, and a wealth of old legends. Its people are reserved and ceremonially courteous.

The picturesque Zakopane ski resort is the winter sports capital of Poland, and it has produced several Olympic champions. Its name means "buried." Zakopane has hosted several international ski championships. Its ski jumps are among the best in Europe. There is a cable-car station near the Kasprowy Wierch, a peak 6,450 feet (1,985 m) high, as well as a speed skating rink. In a good winter, as many as fifty ski lifts are in operation. For Poles, this town in the mountains offers an adventure, with simple accommodation, good company, and perhaps a glass of something warming by the log fire afterward.

WHAT TO DO

Tourists and locals mingle in the historic old town section of Gdansk, a port city on the Baltic Sea.

Public entertainment is expanding. Most towns have a cinema, though almost all the movies come from the United States. Large cities have movie theaters, theaters and concert halls, museums, libraries, and art galleries. Warsaw, Lodz, Krakow, and Poznan are some of the cities with quality theaters and opera houses. Theaters, museums, and everything else close on Monday.

Analog TV has given way to digital across the country. Cable and satellite television give Poles a wide choice of channels, both public and private.

European and American channels such as BBC, HBO, Animal Planet, and Cartoon Network are available in both Polish and English. But some Poles prefer just putting on some music. Music permeates Polish culture. From classical to popular, it is nearly everywhere. American pop is popular.

TOURISM

Freed from state restrictions and aided by improved transportation, Poles are starting to be tourists inside their own country. Visitors from outside Poland come mostly from Germany, by a wide margin. In 2013, German tourists numbered 1,298,702. Next in rank came Russian tourists, numbering 409,243, followed by 380,917 tourists from the United Kingdom.

Whether tourists are from home or abroad, Poland has a wide range of cultural, historical, recreational, and natural destinations. The United Nations Educational, Scientific, and Cultural Organization (UNESCO) has designated fourteen locations in Poland as World Heritage Sites: one natural site and thirteen cultural sites. For example, the entire Old Town of Krakow is on the list, as is the historic center of Warsaw, the medieval town of Torun, the Bialowieza Forest, a castle, several churches, and other historic buildings or landscapes. All of these sites are important tourist destinations. To this list of Polish places of outstanding cultural or natural importance, UNESCO has also added the Auschwitz-Birkenau German Nazi Concentration and Extermination Camp (1940—1945).

AUSCHWITZ One of Poland's top tourist destinations is also the most somber, the German Nazi concentration and extermination camps at Auschwitz. The first camp was constructed by Adolf Hitler's Third Reich to hold Polish political prisoners during World War II. The network of camps quickly expanded to hold thousands of Jews and other people deemed by Hitler to be unworthy of life. More than 1.1 million prisoners died at Auschwitz, 90 percent of them Jews. Of those, some 300,000 were Poles.

Today people from all over the world visit the camps for many reasons. Some may have lost family members there. For others, the camps have become a primary symbol for the Holocaust. People visit to pay respect and come face to face with one of history's most horrific events.

INTERNET LINKS

whc.unesco.org/en/list
UNESCO lists all properties on its World Heritage List by country. Scroll down to Poland and find links to each listing.

www.staypoland.com/poland-attractions.htm
This tourist site offers an in-depth look at ten top tourist destinations in Poland.

www.polska.pl/en
This wide-ranging promotional site has information on tourism, culture, arts, sports, and much more.

FESTIVALS

A huge Christmas tree adorns the city center of Wroclaw.

N ADDITION TO THE YEARLY CYCLE of traditional and national holidays, Poland has festivals, fairs, carnivals, and celebrations galore. Music festivals abound for jazz, rock, pop, classical, and traditional music. There are arts fairs, film fests, book fairs, and food fests, and numerous other kinds of festivities. Many, of course, take place in the summer, when the weather is warm, while others are seasonal.

The ancient cycle of ordained church fasts and holy days dictates the calendar for most Poles. Advent precedes Christmas, which celebrates the birth of Jesus Christ. Ash Wednesday marks the start of Lent, a period of fasting that recalls Jesus' own fast in the wilderness. Palm Sunday welcomes Holy Week, which climaxes on Good Friday and Easter Sunday.

HARVEST FESTIVAL

Harvest traditions are far older than Christianity. Old pagan rituals were discouraged during the Middle Ages, but one that survives is that of the *koza*, or goat. A boy with a sheepskin over his head and shoulders and accompanied by carol singers goes visiting to bring prosperity, help the growth of the corn, and assure a successful harvest. At the harvest home celebrations at the season's end, girls carry the harvest wreath,

12

The town of Kostrzyn, on the Poland-Germany border, hosts the annual Przystanek Woodstock ("Woodstock Poland"), Europe's largest free open air festival that claims to recapture the spirit of the original Woodstock festival held in the United States in 1969.

made of corn and topped with the figure of a rooster or a girl. When the girls finish their special dance, they are supposed to give the wreath to the farmer, and the next year's sowing will start with seed crumbled from the wreath, which is made of last year's crop.

A typical harvest procession today is led by a cross, flanked by choir boys in cassocks and lacy surplices, and followed by the congregation. The procession will visit the fields and barns to thank God for his goodness and ask for his continued bounty.

HOLY WEEK

After the self-imposed disciplines of Lent, the week preceding Easter is a period of varied festivities. Holy Week in Poland is heralded by spring fairs, selling early-grown vegetables and livestock.

These lead into Palm Sunday, a fine reason for the processions Poles love. The palms may be small sprays of everlasting flowers or willow branches mixed with white catkins. In the mountain villages, men make palms up to 15 feet (4.6 m) in height, adorned with flowers, ribbons, and colored papers.

On Maundy Thursday, there may be scenes similar to England's Guy Fawkes bonfires. Some Polish communities take symbolic revenge on Judas Iscariot, hanging a stuffed figure of him, dragging it outside the village, and there burning it or throwing it into the river.

Good Friday is celebrated with solemn services, and then perhaps a visit to a specially created life-size portrayal of the Holy Sepulchre, Jesus' burial place. In Rzeszow, this has become mixed up, in local tradition, with King Jan III Sobieski's victory at the battle of Vienna, so there are Turkish soldiers on guard outside the tomb. Good Friday is a holy day, not a holiday. Some families fast all day.

In Kalwaria Zebrzydowska near Krakow, a spectacular passion play tells the story of Jesus Christ's final hours. The play is as popular locally as the Oberammergau cycle is in Bavaria. The main roles of the play are performed by local priests, while pilgrims play the disciples, Pharisees, and soldiers. They consider this a great honor. Followed by thousands of devout spectators, the play visits over twenty chapels that represent the Stations of the Cross—the highlights of Jesus' path through Jerusalem, carrying the cross to his execution.

On Holy Saturday, homemakers do their Easter baking, and children take baskets of eggs to church to be blessed.

EASTER

The main event of the Catholic year, Easter attracts larger-than-usual crowds to church. The Paschal Lamb, not the Easter bunny, is the focus. Cakes are decorated with a lamb, made either of sugar or wood. The traditional Easter cake is *mazurek* (ma-ZUR-ek), a thin layer of shortbread pastry with different iced flavors, such as chocolate, coffee, and caramel.

Polish children enjoy Easter eggs as much as other children in the world. Eggs are hardboiled and decorated. They are eaten at the Easter breakfast, after Mass. The old way was to boil them with onion skins to dye them a rich

Easter decorations feature a lamb-shaped cake and colorful eggs.

On Easter Monday, the custom of Smigus-Dyngus (water-dousing) provides some light relief. Gangs of children arm themselves with water guns or with buckets and sprays, and roam the streets in search of victims. The boys chase the girls. They might use just a spray of perfume or a plastic lemon as a water gun or a bucket of water. The first one up in the morning is supposed to have the right to spray others, who are not supposed to fight back. (They usually do!)

This custom originated from ritual washing, a purification intended to bring rain to fields sown with grain. Today it is thought of as a damp piece of good luck!

brown. In western Poland, the eggs are stained in a single color; this may be red, yellow, or green. Around Krakow and the south, many colors are used, sometimes with red cutout stencils. In Mazowsze, people cover the eggs with very fine linen, ornamented with the pith from bulrushes.

HIGH DAYS AND HOLY DAYS

On holy days of obligation, Catholics are expected to attend Mass and avoid all unnecessary work. Sunday is a holy day of obligation. There are also ten special days that the Poles call High Days: Christmas, the Circumcision, the Epiphany, the Ascension, Corpus Christi, the Assumption, Saints Peter and Paul Day, All Saints' Day, the Immaculate Conception, and Saint Joseph's Day.

The feast of Corpus Christi honors what is referred to as the real presence of Jesus Christ in the Eucharist, the consecrated bread distributed to

Catholics during Mass. Corpus Christi is observed with colorful processions on the Thursday after Trinity Sunday, with the Corpus Christi, the consecrated bread, held high with great reverence and rejoicing.

Lent, the forty days before Easter, is a time of fasting, when fat, butter, and eggs are forbidden. So on Shrove Tuesday, the day before Lent begins, all these ingredients have to be used up. Pancakes seem an obvious way. In Europe this day is known as Mardi Gras (Fat Tuesday), when people not only feast but enjoy colorful carnivals.

The first day of Lent is Ash Wednesday. During Mass, ashes from the previous year's palms are put in a bowl and sprinkled with holy water. The priest dabs his thumb in the ash and marks a cross on the forehead of each worshiper as a sign of penance.

Lady Day is the traditional name for the Feast of the Annunciation, celebrated on March 25. It recalls how the Archangel Gabriel told Mary of the forthcoming birth of Jesus.

A girl dressed as an angel throws confetti during Epiphany celebrations in Warsaw's Old Town on January 6, 2014.

WESOLYCH SWIAT ("MERRY CHRISTMAS")

Holiday fun for children begins on December 6, St. Nicholas Day. On that day, St. Nicholas visits the children and leaves gifts. In the Wielkopolska region in west-central Poland, the visitor is not Saint Nick, but the Starman. He might first scold the children for misbehavior, and threaten them with a wooden stick or cane, but eventually relents and hands out gifts.

Wiglia (vee-GEEL-yah) (Christmas Eve) is more important than Christmas Day in Polish culture. The eve begins when the first star is sighted. People put on their best clothes, then look for their presents under the Christmas tree.

Children admire the Christmas *szopkas* on display at the annual competition in Main Market Square in Krakow.

A special supper starts with the sharing of bread—the father first, then his family. The meal may consist of fish, noodles, wild mushrooms, cabbage, or herring, but no meat. Alcohol is also not served, because the family will go to the midnight Mass. In some parts of Poland, such as the Silesia region, Baby Jesus or a small angel brings little gifts to children on Christmas Eve.

On the morning of Christmas Day, the family may go to Mass again. Then comes lunch, with rosol, a clear chicken and macaroni soup, and cold meats such as ham and salami, horseradish, potatoes, and salad.

The creche, or *szopka* (SHOP-ka), traditionally consists of puppets or wooden figures representing Herod, the Devil, Death, and the Holy Family in a scene of adoration. A szopka competition is held every year on the Main Market Square in Krakow.

FAMILY OCCASIONS

The big family occasions are baptism, first communion, and marriage. Nearly all Poles receive communion for the first time when they are children. This is a very important event for the whole family, and relations come from all over the country to attend. The children will wear new clothes, often in traditional style.

Wedding anniversaries are carefully noted, because the family unit is very important in Poland. An extra big party is held every ten years. Mother's Day is also very important. Children may perform a play in school and invite their parents. As in many Catholic European countries, birthdays are not celebrated, but Name Days are—they are the feast day of the saint a person is named after.

But Poles don't need an excuse for a party. One father, a twinkle in his eye, explains, "If my boy comes home with a good note from his teacher, then we celebrate. If he comes home without a good note, then the teacher must have forgotten to give it to him, so we celebrate anyway!"

INTERNET LINKS

www.timeanddate.com/holidays/poland
"Holidays in Poland" includes a calendar listing with links to each special day.

sonsofpoland.org/culture-community/polish-customs-traditions
This is an overview of Polish customs and traditions.

www.polishcenter.org/Christmas/CHRISTMAS-ENG.htm
A section about Christmas in Poland, including Advent, Christmas Eve, traditions, and carols.

FOOD

Homemade pickles and preserves are for sale at a local bazaar in the highlands region.

13

NO ONE WOULD EVER ACCUSE POLISH cuisine of being fussy, fancy, or lightweight. This cuisine is meant to stick to the ribs, and while it's there, to fill the stomach and embrace the heart with love as well. As a rule, Poles eat simply but fully. Their style of food is similar to that of many other Slavic nations, and picks up influences from Central European cuisines, as well as Jewish culinary traditions. It is heavy on meat, especially pork and sausages, root vegetables, cabbage, mushrooms, and bread.

Breakfast is usually eaten at around 7 a.m. and is little more than a sandwich with tea or coffee. A second breakfast often follows before midday. This is a light lunch, perhaps including fried eggs and ham or frankfurters, or a plate of cold meats, cheese, rolls, and jam. The main hot meal comes in the late afternoon, and there may be a snack of cold meats or cheese with bread at night. The biggest meal of the week is Sunday dinner, served at noon.

As in other Roman Catholic countries, the traditional Polish Christmas Eve holiday meal is meatless. Called *wiglia* (VEE-gil-yah), the festive dinner typically consists of *barszcz* (beet soup) with small mushroom dumplings, followed by a fish dish such as pickled herring, salads, and sweet poppy seed rolls, gingerbread, and cheesecake for dessert.

BREADS AND CAKES

In Communist times, most of the bread was mass-produced, rather hard, made of rye and often flavored with caraway seeds. Today, more and more private bakeries are providing fancy loaves, croissants, and other breads, as well as the still popular rye. There is a darker brown bread flavored with honey and a white sour rye bread that is good with cheese. Bread is only served in a restaurant if ordered, but Poles eat a lot of bread at home, with butter or margarine, and various kinds of jam, such as plum, strawberry, or blackberry.

A roasted whole carp is a popular dish for the Christmas Eve wiglia dinner.

Cakes are a favorite. Even small villages have their own cake shop. *Sernik* (sir-NEEK), or cheesecake, is popular everywhere, and you may also be treated to poppy-seed cake, sponge cake topped with plums, or marble cake. Festive occasions call for special cakes. Wedding cakes are ring-shaped and studded with round, hard biscuits and decorations made of sweetened dough. For baptisms, cakes are baked 4 feet (1.2 m) long in the belief that the size of the cake will determine the child's happiness and good luck. For funerals, there are special rolls and cakes called *kolaczki* (ko-LACH-kee). Flat pancakes, or *placnik* (platz-NEEK), are made for All Souls' Day, while Easter cakes are flavored with chocolate, coconut, cream, and poppy seeds.

MEAT EATERS

In spite of economic shortages, Poles have remained insatiable meat eaters. Beef and pork are their favorites, with hams and different types of sausages for snacks during the day. The most common meat dish is a fried pork cutlet served in a thick sauce. Because meat is expensive, the average Polish family serves it mostly on feast days or to visitors. Otherwise the menu is vegetable-based and mostly boiled. One favorite meat is Krakow sausage, a special round, brown, very dry sausage, a delicacy with dark rye Polish bread and with beer. Other national dishes are *golabki* (go-WOM-bkee), cabbage leaves stuffed with minced meat and rice; *bigos* (BEE-goss), sauerkraut with spicy meat and mushrooms; *flaki* (fla-KEE), tripe served boiled or fried with carrots and onions; and *golonka* (goh-LON-ka), ham hock with horseradish and potatoes.

Sausages are displayed for sale at a market in Krakow.

Vegetables are usually boiled or mashed potatoes, though there are french fries for tourists, and cabbage, boiled or pickled as sauerkraut. Salads may be simply sliced tomatoes and onions, or thinly sliced cucumbers with dill, lemon juice and sour cream, or grated beets and sour cream. Poles also love potato salad made with mayonnaise, pickles, hard cooked eggs, carrots, and possibly even some chopped apple.

The foundation of Polish cuisine is old Slavic cooking. The Slavs used both sweet and sour cream to make their soups and gravies smooth and piquant as is done in Russian cooking. The widespread use of smoked bacon was typical in what was the East Prussian area of Poland where it was considered almost a sin if a housewife did not fry mashed potatoes in bacon fat until brown, or if she included them in a pot of dumplings. The flavor of smoked bacon and the tartness of sour cream are often blended together in festive veal or beef roasts browned in bacon fat and sauced with cream.

Poles like pickled herring, with onions or in sour cream, particularly between glasses of vodka. In the coastal and mountain areas, people may also eat carp or trout, usually grilled whole to a crispy brown.

EATING OUT

Polish pizza, or *zapiekanka*, is a popular street food. It is an open-faced, grilled baguette with toppings such as melted cheese, mushrooms, and ketchup.

There is a wide selection of eating places in Poland. Quality once varied from day to day depending on the supply of ingredients, but that is no longer a problem. Most expensive hotels and restaurants offer consistently high-quality dining. These are open from late morning to mid-evening. Some do not open until 1 p.m., as alcohol may not be sold before that time.

Cafés are a way of life. They range from cheap soup kitchens, where people munch on sandwiches and drink bottles of very pungent beer, to hotdog stalls, Western-style fast-food outlets, and milk bars, which are often stocked with delicious pastries and ice creams. All the big cities offer a wide range of culinary experiences—from Chinese to vegetarian specialities, and from fast food (such as McDonald's and KFC) to high-priced world-class cuisine.

Along with most other Eastern Europeans, Poles love beets. Beets are a mainstay for the Polish cook. They can be served hot or cold, made into soup or pickled. They are rich in potassium, calcium, and vitamin A.

Beet soups are especially beloved, and include the famous barszcz *(BARshch), or borscht, as it's known to Americans, a clear, spicy red soup served with a dollop of sour cream and fresh dill. Often, it's accompanied by a small meat pastry, such as a sausage roll.* Botwinka *(bot-VEEN-ka) is made from the leaves of baby beet and served with a hard-boiled egg.*

Chlodnik (hwod-NEEK) is a cold pink Lithuanian soup with sour milk and crunchy strips of onion or green vegetables. It looks a little like a strawberry milkshake. Only young beets, both bulb and stem, are used to make chlodnik.

Salads are also made from grated or cubed beet and horseradish. Every Polish vegetable garden will have a few rows of beets for the home larder.

WARMING SOUPS

Polish cuisine is geared to a cold, damp climate. There is a heavy emphasis on soups and meat, especially pork, as well as freshwater fish. Cream is used a lot, and pastries are often rich and delectable. Soup is the start and glory of any good Polish meal. Polish soups range from a light transparent consommé to a rich creamy broth that can be a meal itself. The most popular soup is barszcz, a clear beet soup often served with such Polish favorites as sausage, cabbage, potatoes, sour cream, coarse rye bread, and beer.

Poles also enjoy *zurek*, a creamy, sour, white soup with sausage and potato, and *krupnik* (kroop-NEEK), a thick soup made of barley and potato

Pierogi, or stuffed dumplings, are a favorite Christmas dish. They can be filled with potato, cheese, sauerkraut, or mushrooms.

with pieces of bacon and carrots. Soups are often served with *pierogi* (pyer-OH-ghee), small square pockets of dough filled with a cheesy potato mixture, or mushrooms or cabbage. Pierogi, served as dessert, are filled with fruit or jam.

VODKA AND MORE

For years Poles drank mostly at home, but in cities today, bars have become more popular. Vodka is widely consumed. The Poles claim to have invented the drink, but that claim is hotly disputed by the Russians. Vodka probably originated in the fifteenth century when there was a decline in the supply of honey, the main ingredient in mead, the traditional drink at the time. Someone, either Polish or Russian, experimented by distilling alcohol from grain instead, and vodka was created.

Poles drink vodka in small glasses, tossed straight back. There are many varieties of the drink; some are flavored with bison grass, others with juniper or wild cherry. Regardless, the bottle is supposed to be emptied before anyone can leave. (Modern attitudes about excessive drinking might change this tradition. In any event, children and teens certainly do not partake.)

Beer is mostly bottled. There are several regional varieties. The two most popular brands are the strong tasting Tatra Pils and the lighter Piwo Zywiecki.

Many soft drinks are available too, with strawberry and apple being popular flavors. The better fruit juices are made from real fruit, though there are plenty of cheaper, more chemical concoctions available in cartons. Bottled Coca-Cola and Pepsi are available everywhere. Tap water is not always safe for drinking, so Poles buy bottles of mineral water. There is usually one on the table at any meal.

Poles love tea, or *herbata* (erb-AH-ta). They drink tea with everything, usually in glasses, with lemon and a lot of sugar. Polish coffee is a strong brew, reflecting Turkish influence. It is made by pouring water over ground coffee in a glass or cup. Stirring is not advised, unless you want a mouthful of coffee grounds.

THE POLISH COOK

The Poles have learned through the centuries to be frugal. Until recently, refrigerators were not found in all homes, particularly in the countryside, so food was dried or preserved. The Poles bottle fruit, pickle cabbage and onions, and dry large wild mushrooms. They search the woods for blueberries, believed to be a remedy for failing eyesight, or blackberries. Children sit along the road, selling berries in jars. In the Tatra foothills, people make goat's milk cheese, which is brown-skinned and looks like a small loaf of bread.

A woman sells *oscypek*, a traditional Polish highlander cheese, at a market at a popular tourist resort in Zakopane, in the Tatra Mountains. The cheese is made of sheep's milk and then smoked.

Every home in the village has its own vegetable garden, while an "allotment" on the edge of town serves as a place to grow food crops. In the cities, people check food prices at the supermarket but prefer to buy from a local stall.

In some old countryside homes, food is still cooked on a wood-burning stove topped with an iron plate. The fire below is arranged to provide different cooking temperatures. The center is hottest, for boiling water, and the edges cooler, for simmering soup. The oven section is above the cooking plate and is usually tiled round the sides. This will bake bread, roast meat, and heat the kitchen in winter.

INTERNET LINKS

www.buzzfeed.com/jessicamisener/proof-polish-food-isnt-all-disgusting#.bwrloPvnv
"18 Scrumptious Polish Dishes That Will Rock Your World" is a mouthwatering slideshow.

www.tastingpoland.com/food/list_of_polish_food.html
Tasting Poland offers in-depth information about Polish food with lots of pictures and recipes.

BARSZCZ (BORSCHT, OR BEET SOUP)

1 bone-in meaty beef shank
3 quarts water
1 onion, chopped
1 cup chopped carrots
½ cup chopped celery
3 or 4 dried mushrooms (porcini)
1 bay leaf
3 cups diced peeled beets
2 cups chopped cabbage
¼ cup white vinegar, or to taste
salt and ground black pepper to taste
1 cup sour cream, for garnish
2 tablespoons chopped fresh dill, for garnish

Cook beef shank in a large soup pot over high heat until browned, about 3 minutes per side; add water, onion, carrots, celery, mushrooms, and bay leaf to the pot, add a good dash of salt, bring to a simmer and cook until meat is tender and falling off the bone, about 4 hours. Strain broth, pushing on solids, and then discard solids.

Combine beef broth, beets, and cabbage in a large soup pot; cook, stirring occasionally, until beets are tender, about 30 minutes. Reduce heat to low; add vinegar, salt, and black pepper.

Serve garnished with sour cream and dill.

CHRUSCIKI (POLISH CRULLERS)

Chrusciki (hroos-CHEE-kee) are often made at holiday times.

5 large egg yolks, at room temperature
1 large whole egg, at room temperature
½ tsp. salt
¼ cup confectioners' sugar
¼ cup sour cream (or heavy cream)
1 tsp. vanilla extract
1 Tbsp. rum, brandy, or whiskey
2 cups all-purpose flour
1 qt vegetable oil or 2 lbs. lard
Confectioners' sugar for dusting

Combine eggs and salt in bowl of mixer. Beat at high speed until thick and lemon colored, about 5 minutes. Beat in sugar, sour cream or cream, vanilla and rum. Add flour gradually to form a smooth, soft dough. Add just enough flour so the dough is no longer sticky.

Turn dough out onto a floured board, divide it in half, cover with plastic wrap, and let it rest for at least 20 minutes. Working with half of the dough at a time, roll out to 1/8-inch thickness. These are best when the dough is paper thin. Cut into 1 x 3-inch strips.

Heat 2 inches of oil in a large, deep skillet to 375 degrees F (190 degrees C). Alternatively, melt 2 pounds lard, which is more traditional.

Use a sharp paring knife to cut a slit in the center of each strip of dough, then pull one end through the slit to form a bow.

Fry about 4 to 6 chrusciki at a time (depending on the size of your pan) for just a few seconds on each side. These fry quickly, so watch closely. Do not let them brown. Drain on paper towels. Dust generously with confectioner's sugar.

MAP OF POLAND

Austria, A4, A5, B5

Baltic Sea, A1, B1, C1
Belarus, D1—D3
Beskidy Range, C4
Bialystok, D2
Bielsko-Biala, B4
Biskupin, B2
Bug River, C2, D2—D4
Bydgoszcz, B2

Carpathian Mountains, C4, D4, D5
Chelm, D3
Czech Republic, A3—A5, B4, B5
Czestochowa, B3

Dolnoslaskie, A3, A4, B3, B4

Elblag, C1

Germany, A1—A3
Gdansk, B1
Gdansk Bay, B1, C1
Gdynia, B1
Gliwice, B4
Gniezno, B2

Hungary, B5, C5, D5

Jelenia Gora, A3

Katowice, B4
Kielce, C3
Kolobrzeg, A1
Krakow, C4
Kujawsko-Pomors-kie, B2, C2

Lithuania, C1, D1
Lodz, C3
Lodzkie, B2, B3, C2, C3
Lubelskie, C3, D2—D4
Lublin, D3
Lubuskie, A2, A3, B3

Malopolskie, C4
Mazowieckie, C2, C3, D2, D3
Mazurian Lakes, C1, C2

Neisse River, A3

Oder River, A2, A3, B3, B4
Olsztyn, C2
Opolskie, B3, B4
Ostrowiec, C3
Oswiecim, C4

Plock, C2
Podkarpackie, C3, C4, D3, D4
Podlaskie, C2, D1, D2
Pomorskie, B1, B2, C1, C2

Poznan, B2

Radom, C3
Romania, D5
Russia, C1, D1
Rzeszow, D4

Silesia, B3, B4
Slaskie, B3, B4, C3, C4
Slovakia, B4, B5, C4, C5, D4, D5
Sopot, B1
Swietokrzyskie, C3, C4
Szczecin, A2

Torun, B2

Ukraine, D3—D5
Ustka, B1

Vistula River, B1, B2

Walbrzych, B3
Warminsko-Mazurs-kie, B1, B2, C1, C2, D1, D2

Warsaw, C2
Warta River, A2, B2, B3, C3, C4
Wielkopolskie, A2, A3, B2, B3
Wroclaw, B3

Zachodniopomor-skie, A1, A2, B1, B2
Zakopane, C4
Zamosc, D3
Zielona Gora, A3

ECONOMIC POLAND

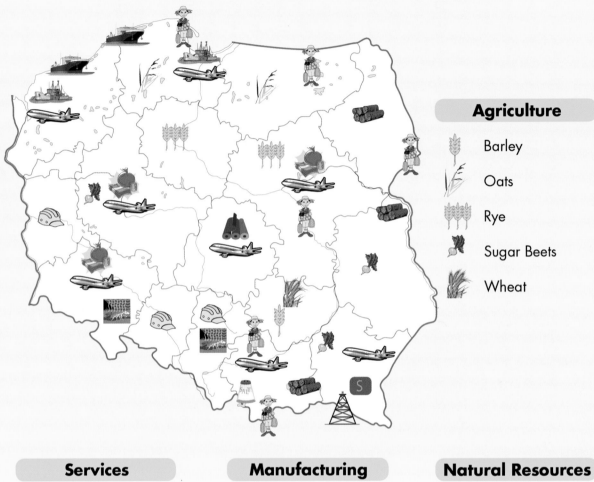

Agriculture

- Barley
- Oats
- Rye
- Sugar Beets
- Wheat

Services

- Airport
- Finance
- Port
- Tourism

Manufacturing

- Forest Products
- Shipbuilding
- Textiles

Natural Resources

- Coal
- Natural Gas
- Oil
- Salt
- S Sulfur

ABOUT THE ECONOMY

OVERVIEW

Poland has pursued a policy of economic liberalization since 1990 and Poland's economy was the only one in the EU to avoid a recession through the 2008—2009 economic downturn. Poland's economy is considered to be one of the healthiest of the post-Communist countries and is one of the fastest growing within the EU. Poles are the second wealthiest, after the Czechs, of the Central European nationalities. Some of Poland's economic challenges include upgrading its road and rail infrastructure, and addressing its rigid labor code, commercial court system, government red tape, and burdensome tax system.

GROSS DOMESTIC PRODUCT (GDP)

US $576 billion (2015)

GDP SECTORS

Services 62.7 percent, industry 33 percent, agriculture 4 percent

WORK FORCE

18.2 million

UNEMPLOYMENT RATE

10.3 percent

CURRENCY

1 zloty (PLN) = 100 groszy
1 zloty = 27 cents; 1 US dollar (USD) = 3.65

PLN (2/2015)
Notes: 10, 20, 50, 100, 200 zloty
Coins: 1, 2, 5 zloty; 1, 2, 5, 10, 20, 50 groszy

AGRICULTURAL OUTPUT

Potatoes, fruits, vegetables, wheat; poultry, eggs, pork, dairy

INDUSTRIAL OUTPUT

Machine building, iron and steel, coal mining, chemicals, shipbuilding, food processing, glass, beverages, textiles

MAIN EXPORTS

Machinery, furniture, foods and meats, motorboats, light planes, hardwood products, clothing, shoes, cosmetics

MAIN IMPORTS

Machinery and equipment, fuels and minerals, chemicals, textiles, metals, agricultural products

MAJOR TRADE PARTNERS

Germany, Russia, France, Italy, United Kingdom, Czech Republic, Netherlands, China, Italy

INTERNATIONAL AIRPORTS

Okecie (Warsaw), TriCity (Gdansk), John Paul II (Krakow)

PORTS AND HARBORS

Gdansk, Gdynia, Gliwice, Kolobrzeg, Szczecin, Ustka

INFLATION RATE

2.25 percent (2015)

CULTURAL POLAND

Sopot
This beach-resort town features Europe's longest wooden pier, a well-loved place for strolls that provides a panoramic view of the town.

Masurian Lakes
A series of interconnected lakes makes this area a great nature stop for activities such as boating, sailing, canoeing, and swimming.

Gdansk
This ancient Hanseatic League city, the birthplace of the Solidarity movement, celebrates Poland's multiethnic past. Gdansk architecture shows significant Dutch and Flemish influence. The port city's symbol is the Neptune Fountain.

Warsaw
Visitors drawn to the capital of Poland for its museums, castles, and beautifully restored old town also have ample opportunities for shopping and dining. Warsaw is also home to one of Europe's finest orchestras.

Torun
The town where Nicolaus Copernicus lived and worked has a university and a museum named after him. The museum —the house he was born in—preserves his revolutionary works on the structure of the universe.

Bialowieza National Park
This primeval forest, home to bison, wolf, lynx, and tarpan ponies, is a World Cultural and Natural Heritage Site preserving a piece of Europe as it was 10,000 years ago.

Poznan
A shopper's delight.

Zamosc
This sixteenth-century town, a World Cultural and Natural Heritage Site, preserves Renaissance architectural traditions in its layout and buildings.

Gniezno
Poland's first capital.

Biskupin
Dating from the Bronze Age, this is the site of an ancient reconstructed wooden fortress of the Lusatian people.

Czestochowa
Poland's religious center is one of the most revered places of pilgrimage for Catholics from all over the world. The Jasna Gora Monastery in Czestochowa houses the Black Madonna, a painting of the Virgin Mary.

Zakopane
Nestled right beneath the Tatra peaks, this mountain-resort town has excellent skiing and hiking terrain and lots of clean, fresh air.

Oswiecim
Visitors to the town known as Auschwitz can enter the concentration camps where the Nazis imprisoned and killed thousands of Jews, Roma, Poles, and others during World War II.

Krakow
Every stone in this city drips with history. The Wawel Cathedral houses royal tombs, and the Kazimierz district, where Steven Spielberg filmed *Schindler's List*, retains its old feel in its Jewish community.

ABOUT THE CULTURE

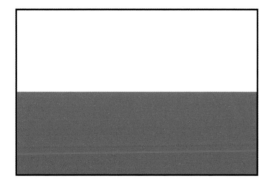

OFFICIAL NAME
Rzeczpospolita Polska (Republic of Poland)

LAND AREA
117,555 square miles (304,465 sq km)

POPULATION
38,346,279 (2014)

CAPITAL
Warsaw

ADMINISTRATIVE DIVISIONS
Zachodniopomorskie, Pomorskie, Warminsko-Mazurskie, Podlaskie, Mazowieckie, Kujawsko-Pomorskie, Wielkopolskie, Lubuskie, Dolnoslaskie, Opolskie, Lodzkie, Swietokrzyskie, Lubelskie, Podkarpackie, Malopolskie, Slaskie

NATIONAL FLAG
White top half, red bottom half

NATIONAL ANTHEM
"*Mazurek Dabrowskiego*" ("Dombrowski's Mazurka")

NATIONAL LANGUAGE
Polish

ETHNIC GROUPS
Polish 96.9 percent, German 0.2 percent, Ukrainian 0.1 percent, other 1.7 percent (2011)

MAJOR RELIGION
Roman Catholicism

LIFE EXPECTANCY
76.6 years; men 72.7 years, women 80.8 years (2014)

IMPORTANT HOLIDAYS
Constitution Day (May 3), National Independence Day (November 11), and all major church feast days

IMPORTANT POLITICAL LEADERS
Lech Walesa—Solidarity leader; president of the Republic of Poland (1990—1995)
Aleksander Kwasniewski—president of the Republic of Poland (1995—2005)
Bronisław Komorowski—president of the Republic of Poland (2010—)
Donald Tusk—prime minister (2007—)

OTHER IMPORTANT FIGURES
Nicolaus Copernicus (astronomer), Marie Curie (physicist), Karol Jozef Wojtyla (Pope John Paul II), Stefan Wyszynski (cardinal), Wislawa Szymborska and Adam Mickiewicz (poets), Frederic Chopin and Witold Lutoslawski (composers), Andrzj Wajda (filmmaker), Artur Rubinstein (pianist), Czeslaw Miloscz (writer)

TIMELINE

IN POLAND	IN THE WORLD
	753 BCE Rome is founded.
700s BCE Celtic groups arrive.	
500s BCE Germanic groups expand from the West.	**116–117** CE The Roman Empire reaches its greatest extent.
500s CE First Slavic groups arrive.	**600** CE Height of Mayan civilization
966 CE Piast rule begins, Gniezno as capital.	**1000** The Chinese perfect gunpowder and begin to use it in warfare.
1038 The capital is moved to Krakow.	
1370 The Piast dynasty ends.	
1385 The Jagellonian dynasty begins.	**1530** Beginning of transatlantic slave trade organized by the Portuguese in Africa.
1572 The Jagiellonian dynasty ends.	**1558–1603** Reign of Elizabeth I of England
1596 The capital is moved to Warsaw.	
1683 Sobieski's army defeats Turks at Vienna.	**1620** Pilgrims sail the *Mayflower* to America.
1772 First Partition.	
1793 Second Partition.	**1789–1799** The French Revolution
1795 Third Partition; last of Polish lands taken	
1830–1865 Various uprisings in Poland.	**1861** The US Civil War begins.
	1914 World War I begins.
1918 A democratic Polish state is created.	**1918** World War I ends.
1919–1920 Polish-Soviet War	
1939 Germany invades Poland.	**1939** World War II begins.

IN POLAND	IN THE WORLD
1944	
Warsaw uprising. Germans level the city.	**1945**
1947	World War II ends.
Poland becomes a Communist republic.	**1949**
	The North Atlantic Treaty Organization (NATO) is formed.
1956	
Industrial strikes in Poznan	**1957**
	The Russians launch *Sputnik*.
	1966–1969
1970	The Chinese Cultural Revolution
Food riots in Gdansk	
1978	
Karol Wojtyla is elected Pope John Paul II.	
1980	
Solidarity strikes in Gdansk. Czeslaw Milosz wins the Nobel Prize in literature.	
1981–83	
Martial law	**1986**
1990	Nuclear power disaster at Chernobyl, Ukraine
Lech Walesa is first freely elected president.	**1991**
	Breakup of the Soviet Union
1997	**1997**
A democratic constitution is adopted.	Hong Kong is returned to China.
1999	
Poland joins NATO.	**2001**
	Terrorists crash planes in New York, Washington, DC, and Pennsylvania.
	2003
2004	War in Iraq
Poland joins the European Union.	
2005	
Poland's president Lech Kaczynski dies in plane crash in Russia.	**2008**
	United States elects first African-American president, Barak Obama.
	2014
2015	Russia invades Ukraine.
Ceremonies mark seventieth anniversary of the liberation of Auschwitz	

GLOSSARY

bigos (BEE-goss)
A favorite Polish dish of sauerkraut, cabbage, mushrooms, onions, and various meats.

collective farming
A system in which a number of farms are run as a unit by a community under state supervision.

communism
A political, economic, and social system in which all property and resources are collectively owned by the state, and wealth is distributed—theoretically—equally or according to need.

European Union (EU)
An economic and political partnership between European nations (twenty-eight as of 2015), created in the aftermath of WWII to foster a sense of interdependence and unity among European nations in order to deter future conflicts.

Flying University
An educational institution founded in Poland in 1882. It did not have a fixed location; instead, classes moved from house to house.

Gorale (goor-A-le)
The Polish highlanders of the Tatra Mountains.

icon
A holy image that is venerated as sacred.

Iron Curtain
The ideological barrier that isolated the Soviet Union and its Communist allies from the West.

Mass
The service in Roman Catholic churches during which worshipers receive the sacrament of Holy Communion.

partition
The division of a country into two or more separate political territories. Poland was partitioned three times in the eighteenth century, until it completely disappeared as an independent country.

Podhale (pod-HA-le)
The meadows in the Tatra foothills where the Gorale live.

resistance
An underground organization fighting for the freedom of their nation.

Russification
Imperial Russia's policy of replacing the native language and culture in education and business with Russian language and culture.

Sejm
Poland's lower house of parliament.

socialism
A transitional stage of society, according to Marxist theory, in which the means of production are state-owned and state-controlled.

Solidarity
The labor movement that became the political opposition to the Communist regime in Poland through the 1980s.

FOR FURTHER INFORMATION

BOOKS

Adamczyk, Wesley. *When God Looked the Other Way: An Odyssey of War, Exile, and Redemption*. Chicago: University of Chicago Press, 2006

Dworak, Marianna. *Authentic Polish Cooking: 150 Mouthwatering Recipes, from Old-Country Staples to Exquisite Modern Cuisine*. New York: Skyhorse Publishing, 2012

Kochanski, Halik. *The Eagle Unbowed: Poland and the Poles in the Second World War*. Cambridge, MA: Harvard University Press. 2014.

Pilecki, Witold. *The Auschwitz Volunteer: Beyond Bravery*. Los Angeles: Aquila Polonica, 2012.

Turp, Craig. *DK Eyewitness Travel Guide: Poland*. New York: DK Publishing, 2013.

Zamoyski, Adam. *Poland: A History*. New York: Hippocrene Books, 2012.

Zeranski, Peter and Laura Zeranski. *Polish Classic Recipes*. Gretna, LA: Pelican Publishing, 2011.

WEBSITES

BBC News. Poland profile. www.bbc.com/news/world-europe-17753718

CIA World Factbook. Poland. www.cia.gov/library/publications/resources/the-world-factbook/geos/pl.html

European Union. Poland. europa.eu/about-eu/countries/member-countries/poland/index_en.htm

Lonely Planet. Poland. www.lonelyplanet.com/poland

President of the Republic of Poland. www.president.pl/en

The New York Times, Times Topics: Poland. topics.nytimes.com/top/news/international/countriesandterritories/poland/index.html

BIBLIOGRAPHY

BBC News. Poland profile. www.bbc.com/news/world-europe-17753718

Carrington, Damian. "Poland's environmentalists fight foresters for heart of primeval forest." *The Guardian*, April 6, 2011. www.theguardian.com/world/2011/apr/06/poland-environmentalists-foresters-primeval-forest

CIA World Factbook. Poland. www.cia.gov/library/publications/resources/the-world-factbook/geos/pl.html

Easton, Adam. "Jewish life slowly returns to Poland." BBC News, April 20, 2012. www.bbc.com/news/world-radio-and-tv-17741185

The Economist. "Shtetl of honour," Oct. 18, 2014. www.economist.com/news/books-and-arts/21625651-new-museum-history-polish-jews-will-intensify-debate-about-how-museums

M.D. "A Golden Age for Polish Farming?" *The Economist*, March 24, 2014. www.economist.com/blogs/easternapproaches/2014/03/polands-agriculture

Ministry of Foreign Affairs, #Poland: Official Promotional Website (beta), www.polska.pl/en/about

Orenstein, Mitchell A. *"Six Markets to Watch: Poland."* Foreign Affairs, Jan/Feb 2014. www.foreignaffairs.com/articles/140336/mitchell-a-orenstein/six-markets-to-watch-poland

President of Poland. www.president.pl/en

Puhl, Jan. "Crisis of Faith: The Catholic Church's Fading Influence in Poland." *Spiegel Online International*, July 12, 2012. www.spiegel.de/international/europe/influence-of-catholic-church-on-the-decline-in-poland-a-843694.html

Reuters, "Polish holders of Swiss franc mortgages chide banks in Warsaw protest," Feb. 28, 2015. www.reuters.com/article/2015/02/28/swiss-snb-poland-protests-idUSL5N0W20GR20150228

Wasilewski, Patryk, and Martin M. Sobczyk. "Polish Government to Close Four Coal Mines, Faces Labor Opposition." *The Wall Street Journal*, Jan. 8, 2015. www.wsj.com/articles/polish-government-faces-opposition-over-plan-to-shut-coal-mines-1420724854

INDEX

FOSSIL RIDGE PUBLIC LIBRARY DISTRICT
BRAIDWOOD, IL 60408

INDEX

3 2186 00216 3326